BRISTOL
AT WORK

BRISTOL AT WORK

JOHN PENNY

breedon books
PUBLISHING

First published in Great Britain in 2005 by

The Breedon Books Publishing Company Limited

Breedon House, 3 The Parker Centre, Derby, DE21 4SZ.

Dedication

Dedicated to all those members of the
Bristol Industrial Archaeological Society
who have worked tirelessly over the years
to preserve the surviving monuments
of our working past.

ISBN 1 85983 355 1

Printed and bound by Cromwell Press, Trowbridge, Wiltshire.

Contents

Acknowledgements

Without the help so generously and freely given by so many individuals and organisations since the early 1990s it would have been impossible to produce this book. The excellent pioneering work on local economic history carried out over the years by the University of the West of England, which has appeared in a variety of forms over the years, has also proved invaluable, and I have drawn heavily upon their expertise in this field. Unfortunately, it is impossible to name all but a few who have provided me with information and illustrations, but special thanks are certainly due to the employees of the Bristol's Museums, Libraries and Record Office, and in particular Dawn Dyer at the Bristol Central Library and Richard Burley at the Record Office. Last, but by no means least, John Bartlett of the Fishponds Local History Society was always on hand to provide help and encouragement, as were various members of the Bristol Industrial Archaeological Society.

Introduction

By the end of the 18th century, in towns and cities up and down the country, there were to be found individuals supplying their populations with the basic necessities of life, and no high street was complete without a butcher, a baker, a grocer, a confectioner, a tobacconists, a draper, a boot maker and other such traditional tradesmen. Likewise, millers, innkeepers and carriers, were also a familiar sight, while carpenters, builders, plumbers, glaziers, wheelwrights, farriers and blacksmiths looked after the fabric of the town and serviced its associated transport, plant and machinery.

Nevertheless, by that time many people were already working for larger undertakings and labour was in great demand, not only on the local farms, estates and smallholdings, but also in the manufacturing and processing concerns that were springing up all over the country. In towns near the sea, or alongside rivers or canals, trades concerned specifically with the water were to be found, while in areas rich in minerals men were required to work in the mines and clay pits or extract stone from the quarries.

Fortunately for Bristol's economic development, its geographical position ensured that a particularly diversified selection of trades and industries grew up over the years, and it was probably during the early 18th century that Bristol adopted its famous motto 'Virtute et Industria', which has been translated as

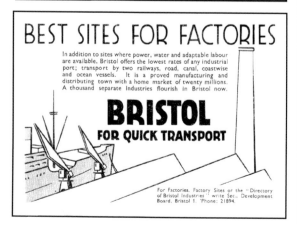

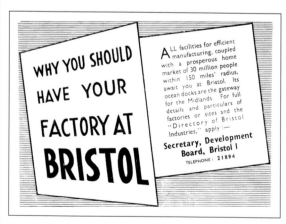

Examples of Bristol Development Board Adverts.

'By Virtue and Industry' or 'Virtue and Hard Work'. Which of the two is closest to the true meaning of those who originally conceived it is of little importance as its message is clear, and over the years the city's skilled and industrious workers have been responsible for producing a range of products, which have been held in high regard throughout the world.

Although this book is only intended as a brief introduction to the fascinating story of Bristol's traditional industries, it will, nevertheless, attempt to describe just how and why certain specialised undertakings became established in and around the city. In spite of the fact that few have survived right through from the 18th century, and that over the years many famous local companies have come and gone and others reinvented themselves or been replaced by those more suited to the times, all have played their part in ensuring the continued economic prosperity, not only of Bristol but also for the surrounding region.

Although the vast number of firms that have existed in the city during the last 250 years has made it impossible to explore the background to all but a handful, it is hoped that those selected will adequately illustrate the diversity of industry that survived in Bristol until the latter half of the 20th century. Many of the accompanying illustrations have been taken from the publicity material circulated at various times by the companies themselves, and hopefully these fascinating advertisements, engravings and photographs will combine with the text to remind people of the undertakings, both past and present, which have helped to establish Bristol as the undisputed 'Metropolis of the West'.

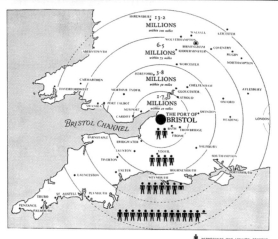

13 MILLION people live within
100 MILES of the Port of Bristol

Excellent communications by rail, road and canal
enable goods to be moved quickly and economically
to and from the Docks at Avonmouth, Bristol
and Portishead

Port of Bristol
QUEEN SQUARE, BRISTOL 1

AVONMOUTH · BRISTOL · PORTISHEAD

Gateway to the World

Bristol has often been described as a 'Gateway City' as not only does it act as such to South Wales, South West England, and the Midlands, but for many years it was an important maritime gateway, first to Ireland, France, and the Iberian Peninsular and later to the West Indies, North America and West Africa. Since its foundation, and indeed right up until recent times, the most important factor in Bristol's evolution has been its port.

For centuries the type of trades and industries in which Bristolians became engaged was dictated by the way in which the port operated, and three basic types can be identified. Of these, the most important over the years for Bristol were the comparatively large concerns dependent upon the importation of raw materials, while of slightly less significance has been the exportation of finished products and servicing the requirements of the port itself. Any study of 'Bristol at Work', however

superficial, must, therefore, begin with an overview of the way in which the Port of Bristol developed and how, over the years, its pattern of trading links has altered.

The Mediaeval Port

Flowing out into the Bristol Channel on Britain's south-west coast is to be found the mighty River Severn, which measuring some 200 miles from source to estuary makes it the country's longest river. Near the mouth of the Severn Estuary the much smaller River Avon flows into it from the east, and some six miles up that waterway it, in turn, is joined by the River Frome. Here, at the confluence of the two, some form of settlement was probably established towards the end of the ninth century. The spot chosen seems to have been at the furthest point downstream where Saxon technology permitted a wooden bridge to be constructed, hence the name Brycgstow, 'the place of the Bridge', which over the years became corrupted to Bristol. Here, as the tide ebbed, the small ships of the time could be easily unloaded as they gently came to rest on the thick mud that ran down from the banks of the river, so establishing the city as a port and setting it on its path to future prosperity.

Over the next few centuries Bristol's increasing wealth was based mainly on its trade with Ireland, but from the mid-12th century increasing amounts of wine from the Gascon port of Bordeaux in south-west France were imported into England. As a result, it was decided to improve facilities in the port, and in the early 13th century quays were constructed on what are now the Welsh and Redcliff Backs, just downstream from the original mud wharves around Bristol Bridge.

However, the little port soon became very overcrowded so, in order to solve this problem, between 1240 and 1247 the River Frome was

A painting of Broad Quay looking towards St Michael's Hill during the late 18th century.

Looking across to Broad Quay with St Stephen's Church in the background, *c.*1865.

diverted into a huge trench some 2,400 feet long, 120 feet wide and 18 feet deep, which was dug in a straight line from the old Frome Bridge opposite St John's Gate, across Canon's Marsh, to link up with the River Avon below St Augustine's Abbey. This had the effect of opening up a whole new reach of the Frome, which then became the city's main port area, and to service it what is now known as Broad Quay was built alongside St Stephen's Church.

During the 14th and 15th centuries Bristol's industrial output steadily increased and trading links were extended to Iceland and the Iberian Peninsular, while from around 1500 local seamen were taking part in voyages of discovery across the Atlantic Ocean. The knowledge they gained, coupled with the foundation of the city's Society of Merchant Venturers in 1551, ensured that Bristol was in the perfect position to exploit the embryonic trade with the New World and later to develop links with West Africa, the Mediterranean and the Baltic.

The Golden Age

The mid-16th century heralded the start of a period of great expansion in trade for the port and ensured that by the start of the 18th century Bristol had entered its greatest period of prosperity. It has been estimated that in 1700 the city contained about 20,000 inhabitants, making it the third largest in England after London and Norwich and securing itself the title of 'Metropolis of the West'. The port of Bristol was even more significant, and at the start of the 18th century it ranked second only to London in terms of vessels, tonnage and men.

As a result of opening up new markets in the North American colonies and the West Indies, funds became available to change Bristol from a mediaeval town to a modern city. The development of this trade also required an extension of the port facilities, and by 1700 the Marsh had become virtually surrounded by stone quays, with the central part being laid out with houses that form today's Queen Square.

Tragically for so many of the victims, part of

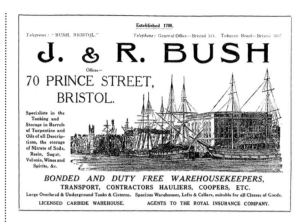

the upturn in trade, which began towards the end of the 17th century, resulted from Bristol slave ships operating the so called 'Triangular Trade'. This involved sailing from the city to the slave coast of West Africa where manufactured goods were exchanged for slaves, which, in turn, were taken on to the West Indies and the North American colonies. Here the slaves were off loaded and replaced with goods such as sugar, rum, molasses, cotton and tobacco, which were brought back to Bristol to feed its rapidly developing manufacturing industries, as well as for onward dispatch.

Nevertheless, by the end of the 18th century the high risks of the slave trade and its growing unpopularity among Bristol's merchants and sailors alike, coupled with keen competition from Liverpool, had undercut the price of Bristol slaves. In fact, the city's share of the volume of the English slave trade in terms of total tonnage declined from 42 percent in 1738 to a mere one percent by about 1803, and within four years it had been partially replaced by the shipping of palm oil from West Africa.

A Floating Harbour

In spite of the fact that the early 18th century has often been called Bristol's 'Golden Age', this period of prosperity was not maintained for long, and by about 1750 the city had in fact been overtaken by Liverpool as the country's second most important port, while by 1801 Bristol was only Britain's sixth largest conurbation in terms of population. Worse still, ships were steadily increasing in size and those entering the River

Bristol City Docks in 1826. Looking down the River Frome towards the River Avon with St Stephen's Church and Broad Quay on the left and the tower of the Cathedral on the right.

An aerial view of the Cumberland Basin showing the entrance and exit locks.

Avon from the Bristol Channel had to contend with seven miles of winding river with fast currents and an exceptionally high tidal range before they reached the quays in the city centre. Bristol was, therefore, forced to plan how to resolve the problems, and between 1804 and 1809 a Floating Harbour was created, which completely transformed the Port of Bristol. Although still centred around the Broad and Narrow Quays, the Grove and the Redcliff and Welsh Backs, the docks had been greatly extended to permanently enclose an area containing some 89 acres of high water, included in which were the new Cumberland and Bathurst Basins.

Unfortunately, in an attempt to recoup some of the money spent on the Floating Harbour project, the Bristol Dock Company introduced extra dues on ships and foreign goods as well as tolls on the new Feeder Canal, which had been cut through to Netham at the head of the tidal reaches of the River Avon. This had the effect of placing Bristol in an unfavourable position when compared with her rivals elsewhere in the country, and by the mid-1820s the charges levied at Bristol on certain selected imports were a little over twice that of Liverpool.

Likewise, by having its trade and industry so geared towards imports, Bristol, unlike its West Coast competitors, developed more as a consumption centre rather than as an entrepôt, with a surplus of mass-produced industrial goods for export. The relatively small quantity and poor quality of local coal plus a lack of a fully developed canal system around Bristol also impeded the process of mechanisation based on steam power, while the small scattered agricultural settlements were unable to provide the labour force necessary for large scale industrialisation. Nevertheless, the period between about 1780 and 1850 is important in that it represents a time of change in the city, and one during which a move was made away from many of the old traditional forms of commercial and industrial enterprise.

Some idea of the variety of work being carried out in Bristol at the end of this period is well illustrated by a piece that appeared in the 'Official Guide to the Great Western Railway', published in 1860: 'This famous old city has been an emporium of commerce for a longer period than almost any seaport in the Kingdom. It long preceded its great rival Liverpool. The existing manufactures of Bristol are numerous and are carried on either within the city or in its immediate neighbourhood, but the manufacturing circuit may be considered to extend six miles around. The principal manufactories are those for glass, sugar, iron, brass, floor cloth, vinegar, tobacco, ship-building, cocoa, carriages, manures, agricultural implements and earthenware.'

Down the Mouth

Although the locks leading to and from the Cumberland Basin were enlarged and realigned between 1849 and 1873, and the following 30 years saw railway lines laid, transit sheds provided and the construction of new quays at Canon's Marsh, Dean's

The Bathurst Basin with the spire of St Mary Redcliff Church in the distance.

A drawing of Avonmouth Dock as it appeared in 1884.

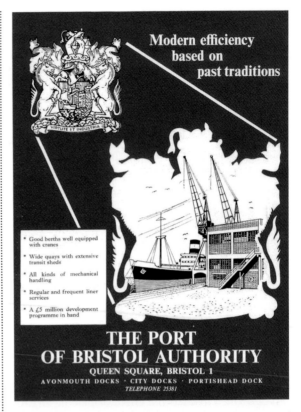

Marsh, Bathurst, Prince's and Wapping Wharves, all these attempts to improve the Floating Harbour were not nearly enough to enable Bristol to compete effectively with Liverpool.

Something much more radical was called for, and since the late 1850s it had been obvious that Bristol's decline as a port could only be halted by the construction of new docks at the mouth of the River Avon large enough to accept modern ocean going ships. After a false start, in August 1868 the Bristol Port Channel Dock Company eventually began to construct a dock covering some 16 acres at Avonmouth, and after toiling for over eight years an army of 'navvies' eventually completed the work, the new dock opening for commercial traffic on 8 April 1877.

Avonmouth Dock in 1901.

An aerial view of Portishead Dock in 1973 showing the Albright & Wilson phosphorous works on the south side and Portishead power station on the north.

However, Avonmouth had not been the location favoured by all, and in 1870 the rival Portishead Port and Pier Company began work on a 16-acre dock at Portishead, on the opposite side of the river mouth. After a number of problems had been overcome, Portishead Dock was officially opened on 28 June 1879, and during the next 30 or 40 years this well equipped facility was used mainly to import wheat, barley and timber, with storage tanks for petroleum being installed in the early 20th century.

With the opening of Portishead, Bristol found itself with three competing dock systems and it is unfortunate that this also coincided with a downturn in world shipping movements. The consequence of this was potentially disastrous as each dock owner attempted to attract trade from the other by slashing its charges to such an extent that none of them could sustain

any degree of profitability. This state of affairs obviously could not be allowed to continue, and in September 1884 the cash strapped Avonmouth and Portishead companies sold out to Bristol Corporation to become part of the Port of Bristol Authority.

However, within 10 years the economic position had changed, and by then Avonmouth was attracting much of the grain trade from the City Docks. Consequently, in 1894 it was decided to

Cocoa beans destined for the Midlands being unloaded at Avonmouth.

An aerial view of the Avonmouth and Royal Edward Dock complex.

Looking across to the Royal Edward Dock showing the Port of Bristol's huge No.5 Granary, which was opened in 1966.

increase its size to 20 acres by adding an extension southwards from the Eastern Wharf. Notwithstanding, trade between Britain and North America being on the increase, Avonmouth was unable to fully exploit this as many of the new steamships coming into service were just too large to pass through the existing lock gates and neither was there any graving dock accommodation.

Various proposals were put forward to solve the problem, but the supporters of an extension at Avonmouth won the day, and so in March 1902 work began on a new ocean liner dock covering some 30 acres to be built on reclaimed and low-lying land to the north of the existing complex. The 1,000 feet long main basin, the dry dock running alongside entrance lock and Junction Cut to link it to Avonmouth Dock took steam diggers only six years to construct, and on 9 July 1908 it was officially opened by King Edward VII, to be known thereafter as the Royal Edward Dock. At the northern end of the main basin two extension arms were later completed, the first to arrive being the Western Arm, which later became the Oil Basin, followed in 1924 by the Eastern Arm to provide additional berths for general cargo.

Due to the small size of the entrance lock, throughout its life Portishead Dock had been relegated to the status of poor relation within the

A low level aerial view of the Royal Edward Dock at Avonmouth.

Port of Bristol. Nevertheless, for many years Portishead's timber business remained fairly constant, while coal began to be shipped in from South Wales following the opening of the adjacent electricity power station in 1929. Albright & Wilson's phosphorous factory was built nearby in 1953, and within 20 years the import of phosphates for the plant accounted for much of the dock's trade.

Traditional trading patterns flourished in the Port of Bristol until the early 1960s, but soon the small coastal vessels, carrying such cargoes as timber and upon which the City Docks depended, were disappearing at a rapid rate. Improved communications were the cause as the newly constructed motorways enabled much of the coastal traffic to transfer to the roads for trans-shipment to continental Europe by modern ferries. At the same time a number of the cargoes were starting to be shipped in containers, and just one of the vessels specially constructed to carry them could hold as much cargo as three or four traditional merchant ships.

Today bulk liquids are handled at Avonmouth, as is timber by Denholm Shipping and domestic

The new headquarters building for the Port of Bristol Authority at Avonmouth. Opened on 2 December 1971, it replaced the existing premises at Queen Square and Avonmouth Dock.

coal by E.H. Bennett Ltd., but many of the well known landmark buildings associated with refrigerated cargoes and the grain trade have been torn down. Some, however, have been replaced by such facilities as Bell Lines container terminal, Bird's scrap metal shredding plant and Castle Cement's installation.

Royal Portbury

Although at Avonmouth extension, adaptation, and major modernisation work has been regularly undertaken over the years in order to keep pace with ever changing commercial requirements, as early as 1967 it had become obvious that in order to attract the new large bulk carriers, tankers, and

The new West Dock photographed in the spring of 1977. It was not renamed Royal Portbury until its official opening by Queen Elizabeth II in August of that year.

On 26 February 1977 the coaster *Edith Sabban* became the first ship to officially enter the new West Dock.

the developing container trade to the Port of Bristol a new dock would be necessary. The only space available for this lay on the estuary flatlands at Portbury, which were located on the southern bank of the River Avon opposite Avonmouth.

In May 1972 construction of what was then known as the West Dock began, and on 8 August 1977 Queen Elizabeth II officially opened the 70-acre basin, thereby chang-

The first commercial ship to use the new container dock at Royal Portbury was the MV *Kiwi Arrow*, which arrived on 12 April 1978.

ing its name to Royal Portbury Dock. Here the trade in forest produce grew steadily, Abbey Hill developed large hard standings to facilitate the importation of cars, and in 1982 United Molasses transferred their storage and distribution plant across from Avonmouth. Redland Plasterboard also built a factory nearby in 1989, as the gypsum they required could easily be imported through the Royal Portbury Dock.

The Demise of the City and Portishead Docks

Unfortunately, back in January 1970, the heavy financial losses the City Docks were suffering forced Bristol City Council to announce that they were to close to commercial shipping. As a result, over the next two or three years fewer and fewer ships used the Floating Harbour, and by 1977 only the little suction dredgers belonging to The Holmes Sand & Gravel Company, which brought

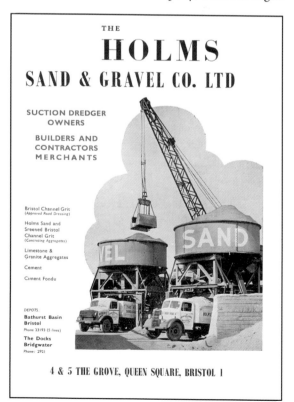

their material up from the bed of the River Severn, were still discharging their cargoes in the centre of Bristol. However, in 1990 even these transferred to Avonmouth, and from then on the Floating Harbour was made over to recreational pursuits.

Down at Portishead trade increased in 1970 when a new terminal was commissioned to handle the import of wood pulp, something previ-

ously undertaken by the City Docks. Unfortunately, this enterprise had a very short life, and due to the availability of more home-produced pulp coupled with the decline of its major customer it was forced to close in 1976. Soon after the power station was decommissioned, and when Albright & Wilson relocated, Portishead Dock was no longer viable, the last ship to use it setting sail in early February 1990.

During the previous 20 years the wind of change had blown strongly elsewhere at the river mouth, for at Avonmouth the grain business had been progressively phased out, while containerisation had effectively ended the traditional frozen meat trade. Across the Avon at Portbury increased costs had prevented the new dock from being fully developed, while in 1986 a downturn in trade led to the twin container cranes being sold to the Middle East. Consequently, the Port of Bristol was in a poor shape financially, and, although the end

One of Albright & Wilson's ships, the 'Bright Pioneer', arriving at Portishead with a cargo of liquid phosphorous from the company's plant in Newfoundland.

such they enjoyed few employment rights in spite of the formation of the Dockers Union in 1887. Neither had much mechanical help provided, and as late as the 1930s the basic tools of the docker's trade were still just the rope, the sling, the shovel, and, of course, the famous steel hand hook used to grasp sacks and crates. Although the work was physically demanding, with the ever-present danger of slipping loads and inhalation of dust from concentrates brought in on 'dirty boats', pay remained poor, and even in 1940 the daily wage of a local docker stood at just 18 shillings.

of the decade saw the beginning of a slow improvement in business, Bristol City Council could not afford to make the major capital investment required to secure the future of the remaining docks.

Nevertheless, the port was far from being a white elephant, as shipping approaching the British Isles from many parts of the world came in via the Western Approaches and thus could dock in the Port of Bristol a day or so earlier than at many of its rivals. In addition, both Avonmouth and Portbury were conveniently situated close to major motorways, while at the latter plenty of space was available for expansion. Fortunately, First Corporate Shipping Ltd recognised the potential and in late 1991 they took a 150-year lease on the docks at Avonmouth and Portbury, with the result that the Port of Bristol Authority ceased to exist, its place taken by the Bristol Port Company, a purely commercial concern.

Dockers and the Dock Labour Schemes

Traditionally, the vast majority of men employed to unload ships in British ports had been casual workers, engaged and paid on a daily basis, and as

Fortunately, for those toiling away in the City Docks or 'Down the Mouth', things began to change for the better following the establishment of the National Dock Labour Board in June 1947. Its main purpose was to register the dockers, provide them with either work or maintenance and by so doing hopefully reduce the number of strikes that regularly crippled the country's docks. In each port a local board with an equal representation of both workers and employers was set up to decide how many registered men would be

Dockers streaming along Gloucester Road, Avonmouth, after finishing work. This photograph appears to have been taken during the 1920s.

required, with the employers paying a levy used to fund their maintenance, as well as a week's paid holiday each year. Nevertheless, stevedores seeking a days work continued to wave their 'black books' at prospective employers from the pens, or 'call-stands' as they were known, located down at Avonmouth or at Prince Street in the centre of Bristol. Although this process resulted in many men still suffering the indignity of being sent

home jobless day after day, the year 1947 did mark the beginning of a process that, 20 years later, culminated in the 'decasualisation' of labour in the Port of Bristol.

This goal was finally achieved in September 1967 when the Dock Workers Employment Scheme was launched, under which the National Dock Labour Board's regional committees were empowered to direct appropriate numbers of men to the organisations and private firms employing stevedores. Locally, the result was that about 700 were allocated to the Port of Bristol Authority, some 350 to Reed & Stock and 245 to

C.J. King & Sons. The dockers thus became full time employees and, thereafter, enjoyed the same security of employment and fringe benefits already taken for granted by most other workers. Although this did much for labour relations, such problems continued to exist in the docks and a particularly disruptive tally clerk's strike at the Dublin terminal at Avonmouth in 1981 effectively put an end to over 150 years of trade with Ireland.

However, further difficulties centred around the growing amount of surplus labour in the industry were averted when the findings of the Aldington-Jones Commission paved the way for the introduction of the Dock Work Regulation Act of 1976. This led to the phasing out of the National Dock Labour Board in 1989 and of many long serving dockers electing to accept the very generous redundancy terms on offer. These men were soon replaced by newly trained workers known as port operatives, and the removal of restrictive practices meant that even office staff might be drafted in to assist with unloading ships when the need arose. A complete revolution in working practice had taken place, which, coupled with the investment of millions of pounds by the Bristol Port Company, effectively reversed the large losses made while the docks were under Council control and in so doing gave Bristol a port fit for the 21st century.

CHAPTER 2
Coal Mining and Quarrying

The Bristol Coalfield

As a factor in the economic development of Bristol since the 18th century, the availability of coal was second only in importance to the port itself. Just as the River Avon provided the artery up which raw materials flowed into Bristol from various parts of the world, the existence of a local coalfield enabled the city to make full use of these, and thus Bristol become industrialised even before the start of the Industrial Revolution proper.

The fact that no other city in southern England was situated on a coalfield made Bristol an ideal place to undertake manufacturing. Consequently, by the mid-18th century the city was already engaged in the production of glass, sugar, soap and pottery, as well as working with metals such as brass and lead. All of these industries consumed a great deal of coal, and by 1750 there were over 140 collieries operating in the Bristol area, allowing annual production to reach about 14,000 tons by 1790.

Geographically, the coal bearing rocks occur locally within a triangular area bounded by Cromhall in Gloucestreshire and Frome and Nailsea in Somerset, but over a large part of the area they are obscured by sandstone and clay. Historically, the Bristol coalfield was one of the first in Britain to be exploited, and the earliest workings were on the outcrops, particularly around the Kingswood Forest in the parishes of Bitton, Hanham, Stapleton, Westerleigh and Mangotsfield.

During the 1740s a coal mining surveyor, at that time busy working in the Kingswood area, discovered similar geological structures in and around Bedminster, and in order to begin developing the new coalfield he went into partnership with Jarrit

---

STAPLETON,

AUGUST 10, 1792.

AT a Meeting held this Day of US, the underſigned PROPRIETORS and OCCUPIERS of COLLIERIES in *Kingswood, Lower-Easton,* and *Bedminster,* it was unanimouſly agreed,

That in the preſent Circumſtances of our reſpective Workmen, many of whom have been forcibly taken from their Work, and others have violently prevented any Colliery from being worked, in open Violation of the Laws, we cannot enter into any Conſideration of the Propriety of the Claims ſet up for an Advance in Colliers' Wages, and in the Price of Coal : But that when thoſe Perſons now out of Employ ſhall have peaceably returned to their reſpective Works, and ſhall have laid before their reſpective Employers (which they have never yet done, either before or ſince their leaving their Work) any reaſonable Propoſals for a Riſe of Wages and Price of Coal, we will be ready and willing to liſten to the ſame, and ſhall have great Satisfaction to find that ſuch an Accommodation can be made as will inſure to the Workman the fair Reward for his Labour, and to the Coal-Owner ſuch a reaſonable Profit as the preſent Demand for the Commodity will bear.

Charles Bragge,
Charles Arthur,
John Whittuck,
John Tippett,
Solomon Leonard,

Moſes Rennolds,
Nicholas Harriſon,
Thomas Jefferies,
Samuel Tippett,
Jacob Selwood Riddle.

A handbill prepared by coal pit owners in North East Bristol during a wages dispute in August 1792.

Smyth, the local Lord of the Manor, to form the Bedminster Coal Company, and it was not long before pits were springing up all over the district.

The Kingswood & Parkfield Colliery Company

Although during the 19th century the Bristol coalfield continued to expand, it did loose some of its previous status as a result of a marked reluctance on the part of many mine owners to modernise their operations. To add to the problems, the local seams tended to be thin and relatively difficult to work, while by the middle of the century many of the upper veins had been worked out. So, in order to keep up with demand it became necessary to exploit seams that lay at greater depth and this, of course, required considerable capital investment. However, as it was difficult for individual owners to raise the sums necessary they started to consolidate their holdings and, as a consequence, although production in Kingswood and South Gloucestershire reached its peak in 1879, by then there were just 21 working collieries.

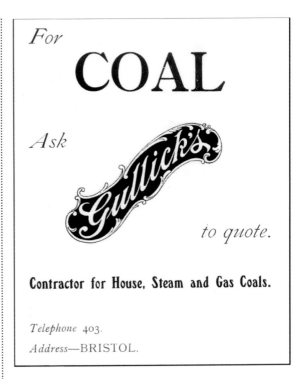
The fact that the area's full potential was realised during the second half of the 19th century was due to the genius of a self taught geologist and local entrepreneur named Handel

Parkfield Colliery photographed in around 1895.

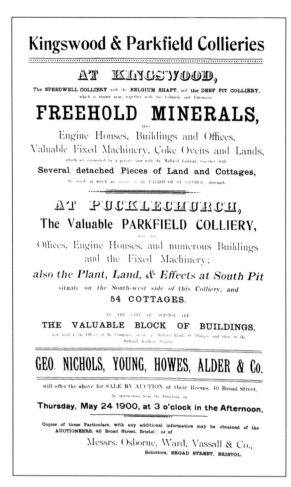
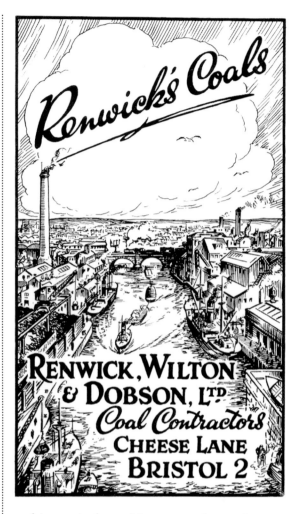
Cossham, the son of a carpenter and joiner, who was born in Thornbury in 1824. Although a man of extreme views, he was also a dedicated nonconformist whose lifelong purpose as he saw it was to do 'all the good I can, to all the people I can, in every place I can, throughout life'. This attitude endeared him to many in the local community and in particular to his own employees. In 1845 he became a clerk at the colliery on Yate Common and while working there undertook the diligent study of mining, geology, science, architecture and engineering. His studies culminated in a systematic investigation of the geological structure of

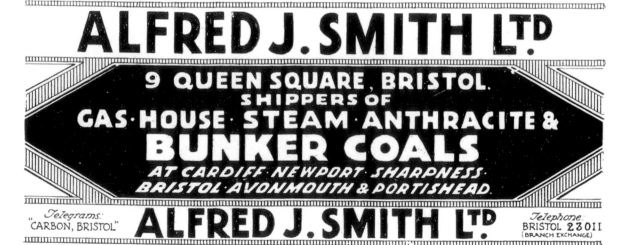

the northern edge of the Kingswood anticline, where he discovered hitherto unknown coal seams, which he went on to so successfully exploit.

Handel Cossham married Elizabeth Wethered in 1848 and entered into partnership with her father, William, and her three brothers, Joseph, Henry and Edwin, to lease the Brandy Bottom colliery and nearby abandoned pits at Parkfield, near Shortwood, from the owners Sir John Henry Greville Smyth and C.E.H.A. Colston. Here they intended to develop a new mine, which was to be known as Parkfield Colliery. Cossham was placed in charge of the day to day running, and operations began in 1851, two shafts 280 yards deep subsequently being sunk. In 1857 some 69,000 tons of coal were raised from the new colliery, although full production was not achieved until 1860 when 111,000 tons were extracted. From then until 1879 output fluctuated between 110,000 and nearly 156,000 tons, the maximum occurring in 1875, some two years after a new shaft was opened at Brandy Bottom, which by then was usually referred to as Parkfield South.

However, by that time Cossham had already

turned his attention to Kingswood, where he not only went on to establish his reputation but also made his fortune. He first became involved with Kingswood back in 1863 when Cossham and Wethered began leasing two mines from William Chester-Masters, the shaft at Speedwell being some 1,140 feet deep and that at Deep Pit, 1,230 feet. These were fairly old workings, having been known respectively as Starveall and Tylers during the last decade of the 18th century, worked by the Brian family from 1822 and linked underground by 1850. In spite of the fact that by the time Cossham took over the pits they were considered to be almost exhausted, his geological discoveries and subsequent development work soon made the Kingswood collieries the most important in both size and output in the Bristol area.

In 1867 a further lease was obtained from Chester-Masters and the partners floated the Kingswood Coal and Iron Company, with Cossham and Wethered as directors. To consolidate his interests further, in 1875 Cossham purchased the Duke of Beaufort's mining interests in the parish of Stapleton, as well as Chester-Masters mineral rights in St George, and when the Wethered family sold out to him four years later he formed the Kingswood and Parkfield Colliery Company Ltd. Now that Cossham had full control of the collieries he began a programme of modernisation and expansion that brought him his personal fortune. By 1886 he was extracting between 700 and 1,000 tons of steam and house coal per day from recently discovered veins, which enabled the life of some of the existing coal mines in the Bristol area to be extended well into the 20th century. At the time of Handel Cossham's death in 1890 his company owned some 3,000 acres of mineral freehold, together with four collieries, Parkfield, Parkfield South, Speedwell and Deep Pit, which employed a total of around 1,500 men, making it the largest employer of labour in the West of England.

The maximum output by local pits was achieved between 1870 and 1880, so the end of Cossham's life also coincided with the start of a steady decline in the coal mining industry in the

The Cossham Memorial Hospital, Kingswood Hill, opened in June 1907.

Bristol area. Nevertheless, although Cossham's discoveries had prolonged the life of the industry, it was clear to those connected with the local mines that their demise would come sooner rather than later, particularly as the coalfield had underground problems that could not easily be overcome. The thinness of the seams, some of which were also of poor quality, the complexity of the geological features, which often necessitated deep workings, and the difficulty of drainage all conspired against those attempting to extract coal and raised the cost of production. Consequently, the local industry found it increasingly difficult to face the competition from outside the area that began to make an impact following the opening of the Severn Railway Bridge at Sharpness in 1879. It was, however, the arrival of the Severn Tunnel in 1885 that finally brought the South Wales collieries and their high quality products within easy reach of Bristol.

A staunch Liberal and enthusiastic lay preacher, Handel Cossham had been a very com-munity-minded man, and during his life had been not only a County Councillor but also MP for East Bristol and served two terms as Mayor of Bath, his private residence being at Weston Park, just outside the city. A considerable portion of his wealth was also spent for the benefit of local peo-ple, and in particular his own employees. Not only did he set up schools for his miners' children but he also advocated the introduction of pithead baths, decent housing, the use of enclosed cages and lined shafts and commissioned detailed research into efficient ventilation methods. Throughout his career, Cossham believed that the only real way to prevent accidents was 'to educate the miners in the ways and techniques of mining', and as a way of accomplishing this he made him-self the prime mover in the establishment of the Bristol Mining School in Nelson Street.

Handle Cossham died on 23 April 1890, and such was the esteem in which he was held in East Bristol that between 40,000 and 50,000 people gathered in and around Avon View Cemetery. His good works even continued after his death, and after his wife had died and his former properties sold the proceeds were used to endow the Cossham Memorial Hospital, which was built on Kingswood Hill. It opened in June 1907, but ironically the first inquest held there was on a young man killed in an accident at Hanham Colliery.

Mines to the North and Mines to the South

Cossham's main rival, working in the northern part of the Bristol Coalfield, was Leonard, Boult & Company Ltd, an undertaking that went on to own a number of important mines in the area. The best known of these was probably the Easton Colliery, which had originally been sunk around 1830 by Messrs Davidson and Walter, its shaft eventually reaching a depth of over 1,000 feet. In 1849 the proprietors amalgamated their interests with that of Leonard, Betts and Boult, owners of a nearby pit, the new firm being known as the Easton Coal Company, before, in 1854, the concern was retitled Leonard, Boult & Company, finally acquiring limited liability status in 1880.

Over the years the firm went on to exploit and develop a number of local collieries and in 1860 were responsible for sinking the shaft for the new Whitehall colliery, after which a travelling way was driven between it and their Easton pit. Further expansion took place in 1872 when Leonard, Boult & Company purchased the Jefferies Hill pit at Hanham from Mr J.J. Whittuck, and over the next 15 years considerable improvement was undertaken in order to satisfy

demand for its excellent quality coal. Unfortunately, the company failed during the mid-1890s and, following liquidation in 1896, Messrs Powley & Thomas, a South Wales based mining concern, formed a new firm, the Bristol United Collieries Company, to run Easton, Hanham and Whitehall.

South of the River Avon in the Bedminster and Long Ashton areas, the longest established coal mining concern was the Bedminster Coal Company, proprietors of the Dean Lane Colliery, which had in fact been the first mine that they had developed back in the mid-18th century. In later years the South Liberty pit was acquired by the Ashton Vale Iron Company Ltd, who were also the proprietors of the nearby Ashton Vale Colliery. The sale of the South Liberty pit allowed the Bedminster Coal Company to concentrate all their efforts at their Dean Lane pit, and, consequently, here the shafts were deepened and the workings eventually extended as far north as Barton Hill.

Leonard Boult & Company's Easton Colliery during the late 19th Century.

Also to be found south of the River Avon was the Malago Vale Coal Company, which, by the mid-1870s, was employing about 400 men, making it the next largest coal concern after Cossham's firm. The original shaft at the Malago Vale pit had been sunk in about 1840 and by 1854 was being worked by Steedes & Pilditch, by 1874 by the Malago Vale Coal Company itself and finally from around 1877 by Bristol Collieries Ltd. It was, however, not to survive into the 20th century, its final demise being brought about by an industrial dispute in which the miners demanded 1d per hour compensation for loss of earning caused by the inconvenience of working with safety lamps introduced following a recent explosion. This the management refused to grant, and, following a strike that was to last for some 15 months, in 1892 all 300 workers were finally laid off and the mine closed.

Following Handel Cossham's death, it took a considerable time to sort out his estate, and it was not until 1900 that Parkfield, Parkfield South, Speedwell and Deep Pit were finally put up for sale, the purchasers being a consortium known as the Bedminster, Easton, Kingswood and Parkfield

A close up view of South Liberty Colliery early in the 20th century.

The South Liberty Colliery in Bedminster.

Underground at South Liberty Colliery.

Collieries Ltd, which had been formed to amalgamate the larger mining concerns in the Bristol area. As a result, the group took control of the old Bedminster Coal Company's Dean Lane colliery, the Easton, Hanham and Whitehall pits, until recently grouped together as the Bristol United Collieries, in addition to the four mines belonging to the Kingswood and Parkfield Colliery Company Ltd.

Its headquarters was initially established at the Dean Lane Colliery, and, not surprisingly, John and Alfred Bennett, two of the three directors appointed to run the new concern, had previously been connected with the Bedminster Coal Company. As a single group now owned many of the mines still operating on the Bristol coalfield, the galleries of those located north of the River Avon were connected so that it would have been quite possible for a miner to walk entirely underground from St Philips to Kingswood!

A number of smaller operators were still busy extracting coal in the Bristol area, notably the Ashton Vale Iron Company Ltd at Bedminster and the Frog Lane Colliery at Coalpit Heath, where development work had been started in about 1852 by the Coalpit Heath Coal Company. Formed back in the 18th century by a partnership between the landowner, Sir John Smyth, and two minority shareholders, throughout most of its long life the company managed to remain independent.

The Decline of the Local Collieries
In spite of cost saving amalgamations, by the dawn of the 20th century the Bristol coalfield was actually in terminal decline, increased competition and rising costs having resulted in the annual

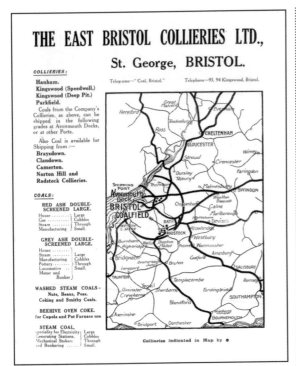

average output falling from 524,156 tons in the 1870s to 43,697 by 1900. This, of course, resulted in further closures and layoffs, the first of these occurring in August 1906 when the Ashton Vale Colliery closed and 184 men were thrown out of work. Not long after, production also ceased at the nearby Dean Lane Colliery, after which Lady Smyth arranged for the five-acre site to be cleared by unemployed men before, in 1910, she presented it to the City Council, which subsequently laid it out as the Dame Emily Smyth Park. Further closures followed in June 1911 when work stopped at the interlinked Whitehall and Easton collieries, while in 1914 Bedminster, Easton, Kingswood and Parkfield Collieries Ltd itself was put up for sale. However, as a satisfactory offer was not received a new concern known as the East Bristol Collieries Ltd was subsequently floated.

World War One gave the remaining pits some-

A photograph of Speedwell Colliery taken shortly before it closed in 1936.

last mine south of the River Avon, was finally forced to close. The following year the Hanham pit was shut, while production ended at Deep Pit in 1928. This left just Parkfield, Speedwell and Coalpit Heath to soldier on, although by the early 1930s many of the upper coal seams were becoming exhausted and water ingress into the deeper workings was presenting an increasing danger.

In spite of this, in 1933 the people of Bristol went as far as subscribing £3,000 towards new exploratory borings, and although the East Bristol Coal Company subsequently identified the existence of coal bearing seams, unfortunately, they were too deep to be worked economically. To compound the difficulties, orders from the power stations were also dropping off, leaving the East Bristol Coal Company Ltd with little option but to stop production, consequently in 1936 both Parkfield and Speedwell closed, a move that adversely affected the livelihoods of nearly 1,000 men.

By contrast, the Frog Lane Colliery at Coalpit Heath was still a viable proposition in spite of the increasing shift towards the use of gas and electricity, both in the home and by industry, and upon nationalisation in 1947 the 258 underground workers succeeded in extracting some

thing of a reprieve, but once the conflict was over their futures became increasingly uncertain due to many energy users starting to switch over to oil. Rationalisation of the coal industry in the Bristol area soon followed, and in 1925 South Liberty, the

Deep Pit Colliery at Crofts End taken in 1899.

Underground working at Frog Lane Colliery, Coalpit Heath, in about 1905.

Frog Lane Colliery, Coalpit Heath, photographed in about 1905.

3,500 tons of coal. Nevertheless, two years later it too succumbed when rising water levels caused by an ingress of water from the abandoned Parkfield workings forced the pumps at the last deep mine in the area to give up the unequal struggle.

This having been said, a final attempt to revive the local coal industry was made by the National Coal Board in 1952 when work started on the development of an experimental drift mine at Harry Stoke, just north of Bristol. Here, two drifts were sunk and coal extraction began in 1954. If all had gone well it was intended that a pair of shafts would be sunk when the drifts reached the deeper measures, thus heralding the start of a major development scheme. Unfortunately, that plan never came to fruition as geological problems conspired to render the colliery uneconomic, the NCB finally closing it on 14 June 1963 and with it a long chapter in the history of Bristol at work.

At the same time, and accelerated by the Government's establishment of smokeless zones, the domestic and industrial coal distribution network also began dramatically reducing in size, and soon many long established firms, the names of which had for generations been familiar to Bristolians, began to disappear as the switch to fuels such as gas, oil and electricity gathered pace.

Until the first half of the 19th century coal miners received wages roughly in line with those being paid to other unskilled or semi-skilled workers, but, unfortunately for local men, the pay in the Bristol coalfield was always below that on offer elsewhere in the country. By 1840 an adult collier could expect to receive between 18 shillings and £1 for a full weeks' work, with lads aged between 14 and 18 having to manage on seven to 12 shillings and those under 13, two to six shillings. Unionisation on a national scale took some time to achieve, and it was not until 1889 that the Miners' Federation of Great Britain began to attract the support of most local organisations, including the Bristol Miners' Association. Its formation came none too soon as although the 1890s saw a fall in the price of coal that in turn led to a reduction in wages, the union countered by demanding shorter working hours. This campaign was successful, and in 1908 the government introduced the Eight Hour Bill, which, as its name suggests, gave the miners an eight-hour working day, although 'winding time' was not included. To implement this the pits normally worked a two-shift pattern, the first being from 6am to 2pm and the second from 2pm to 10pm.

Wages, of course, were still the union's main concern, both at a national and a local level, and the first three decades of the 20th century were dominated by the struggle to stop the mine owners cutting the men's pay. By the early 1930s colliers in the Bristol area had been forced to accept a reduction so the flat rate for six days work stood at just £1.19s.10d, a figure below the subsistence level set by the Poor Law authorities!

Fortunately for those who had to labour in the pits, in the Bristol area they were mainly non-fiery. Consequently, explosions caused by the build-up of Methane gas were so rare that for many years the miners used candles in their hats for illumination, a good example being at Speedwell where safety lamps did not finally replace naked lights until 1928. Locally, the miners lot was always an unpleasant one as seams of

The Harry Stoke drift mine, photographed in 1960.

the district were much narrower than most of those worked in other parts of the country, causing extremely cramped working conditions. Although there was little to fear from explosions, death from a variety of other accidents were not uncommon, while there was always the risk of suffocation due to the inhalation of 'blackdamp', something that the colliers had to be aware of right up until the closure of the area's last pits.

Stone Quarrying

Closely associated with the coal measures in the Bristol area is the famous Bristol pennant stone, a hard sandstone that occurs either with a pleasing blue colour or as a slightly harder pink coloured stone, known locally as Red Pennant. Over the course of many generations, the value of this material was appreciated by builders, architects, surveyors and engineers alike, who used it for a variety of purposes, and for centuries many buildings erected in the Bristol area were constructed using pennant stone. Although brick and other materials gradually displaced pennant in house and wall building, up until World War Two it was still being widely employed for such things as street kerbs and paving stones as it is very durable and is not slippery when worn. Similarly, its weather-resisting properties, uniformity of colour and very fine grain have also endeared it to monumental masons over the years.

Quarries producing pennant were concentrated in the north of the Bristol coalfield, with the vast majority being located in, or near, the side of the valley of the River Frome, in Fishponds, Stapleton, Frenchay and Winterbourne. It was

also extracted elsewhere in the vicinity, notably at Easton and Crew's Hole. The quarries themselves were usually nothing more than large holes in the ground with inferior stone near the top layers, but with fine layers of Bristol pennant to be found in heavy seams up to eight feet deep lying from a depth of about 30 feet down to as far as it was practical to extract the stone.

In 1858 there were about 16 pennant quarries in operation north of the River Avon, and their total annual production amounted to over 24,000 tons. The main products at that time were paving stones, block stones for facing buildings and rough house building stone. By 1890 this number had dropped to about eight, but the industry was still being run by individual quarry masters in direct competition with each other. However, the situation changed dramatically early in the last decade of the 19th century when many English towns began opening up new housing developments and expanding their streets and roads. This led to a period of prosperity for the local quarries,

Quarrying in the Bristol area early in the 20th century.

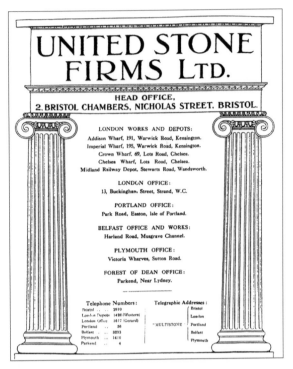

and large orders soon began to arrive, particularly from places near London were there was no naturally occurring hard stone.

In order to meet the sudden upsurge in demand, a number of quarry masters felt it advis-

able to combine together to form a limited liability company, so as to be able to pool their resources and induce some badly needed capital, which could be used to purchase new plant and finance their operations. Consequently, in 1895 Thomas Free & Sons, John Grant, Jacob Monks & Sons, George Parker, and Fred Greenway formed a company called The Bristol Pennant Stone Firms Ltd, which had its headquarters in Fishponds. Thomas Free was appointed general manager and John Grant and Fred Greenway acted as assistant managers, responsible for the supervision of the group's seven quarries. Unfortunately, Jacob Monks and George Parker insisted on being paid in cash for their interests rather than leaving the balance of the capital for future development, and this ensured that the firm was not properly financed and soon ran into difficulties.

One way to ease the problem was by further amalgamation, and in 1896 the first steps were taken to combine the Bristol Pennant Stone Firms Ltd with not only the Bath Stone Firms, a highly successful and profitable company handling the famous Bath Stone, but also with the De Lank Granite Company of Cornwall and the Keinton Stone Company and Joseph Seymour (Street), both based in Somerset. The new group, called the Hard Stone Firms Ltd, had adequate capital, and with the directors of the Bath Stone Firms being the majority shareholders they immediately moved the headquarters to Bath and altered the organisation and management arrangements.

Further amalgamation with other quarry concerns well outside the Bristol area took place in 1909, the subsequent conglomerate being named United Stone Firms Ltd, which had its head office in St Nicholas Street, Bristol. Financial problems in the 1920s led to a new company, United Stone Firms (1926) Ltd, being formed, but neither this concern nor others such as the Bryant & Langford Group of Quarries, which existed between about 1927 and 1934 and had a quarry at Winterbourne, was able to stem the decline in the use of Bristol pennant stone. Consequently, by 1939 quarrying in the East Bristol area had all but ceased, the only short-lived exception being Thomas Free & Sons

Limestone quarrying in the Avon Gorge in 1733.

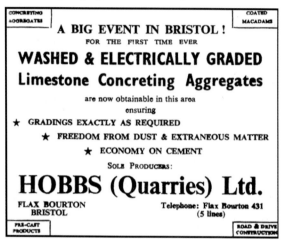
Ltd at Frenchay. In their quarry the normal working week at the start of World War Two comprised some 48 hours, with skilled masons and markers out receiving 1s 5d per hour, cutters, hole makers and quarrymen, 1s 3d, and labourers, 1s ¾d.

Not only has pennant stone been quarried in and around Bristol, but the deposits of carboniferous limestone found on or near the sides of the valley of the River Avon in the area around the Avon Gorge and the Downs have also been exploited over the years. Here during 1856 the Black Rocks, Durdham Down and St Vincent quarries produced over 60,000 tons, the stone being sold for between 10d and 1s 6d per ton. As well as being burnt to make lime, it was also used for road making, sea wall pitching and, in polished form, to adorn the new Oxford University Museum of Natural History and the Houses of Parliament in London. Today local limestone is still being exploited commercially, although the industry is now concentrated slightly to the south of Bristol in the Flax Bourton area.

The Local Potteries

Another local industry, which for many years depended upon the Bristol coalfield for its fuel, was the pottery industry, an activity that also made extensive use of the locally occurring coal measures clay that occurs in large amounts in an area stretching from Bedminster north-east to Kingswood and beyond. Here generations of men toiled away in pits to dig out clay or claystone, which was then crushed into a fine powder and mixed with water to make a material suitable for moulding into all types of pottery. However, as the public demand for more sophisticated tableware grew, those local manufacturers engaged in its production were forced to import more suit-able clay from outside the area, and this expensive inconvenience was one of the reasons for the area's last surviving pottery relocating to Cornwall, the main source of its raw material.

Although mediaeval-style, rough lead-glazed wares were made in Bristol for many hundreds of years, it was the introduction of an opaque, white tin glaze that revolutionised the pottery trade in Britain, and locally the manufacture of this enamelled earthenware, known today as 'Bristol Delft', began in the early 1650s. Bristol was also involved in the development and manufacture of porcelain from about 1746, although it ceased in 1778 when production was moved to Staffordshire. Nevertheless, the pottery industry in the city continued to develop, and from the 1780s those firms previously satisfying the demand for domestic crockery began switching over from making tin-glazed earthenware to manufacturing creamware, a move made possible by the introduction of a transparent lead glaze.

Bristol remained an important pottery centre throughout the 19th century and well into the 20th, during which time local companies tended to concentrate on producing redwares and in particular stoneware. In fact, Bristol stoneware, with its famous impervious glaze, was such an important invention that it soon became used through-

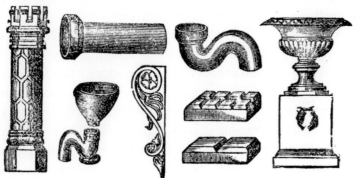

Part of the workforce at the Fishponds & Bedminster Brick and Tile Company's works in Ridgeway Road, Fishponds. This photograph was taken during the late 19th century.

out the country, while in the city itself numerous potteries were at one time engaged in its manufacture. Unfortunately, economies of scale ensured that it eventually became impossible for the relatively small Bristol firms to compete with large-scale manufacturers from outside the area. Consequently, only Pountney & Company Ltd producing earthenware, Price, Powell & Company making stoneware and the Hollychrome Bricks Ltd were still in business by the 1960s.

J.D. Pountney's Temple Back Pottery in 1820, with Temple church in the background.

The Bristol Pottery - Pountney & Company Ltd.

Many potteries flourished in the Temple and Redcliff areas during the 18th and 19th centuries, but the Bristol Pottery was the longest lived of all the local earthenware producers and the one that prided itself on being the oldest pottery manufacturer in Britain. Its long and complex history can be traced back to the Brislington Pottery, built on the site of the old mediaeval chapel of St Anne, where in the early 1650s its workers began making delft ware. In about 1683 the proprietor, Edward Ward, a noted Anabaptist, established the Temple

Back Pottery at Water Lane in Bristol, from where, after 1697, he and his three sons worked exclusively until his death in early 1710.

For a short time the pottery was in the hands of Edward's son, Edward Ward junior, but after he died in 1712 it was passed on to his two daughters, whose guardian was their uncle, James Ward. During his period at the helm the quality of workmanship gradually improved, and he was soon employing some of the best artists of the period. However, in about 1732 he handed over the Temple Back Pottery to his son, Thomas Ward II,

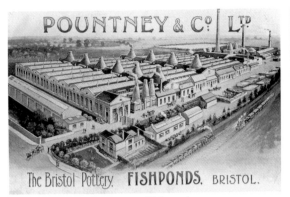

Pountneys' Bristol Pottery at Fishponds.

in order to concentrate on another business he was running in partnership with the husband of his only surviving niece, the lady who also owned the pottery.

Although Thomas Ward II died in 1738, his widow, Frances, continued his work, taking several pupils on between 1739 and 1741. However, she died shortly after, and in 1746 Thomas Cantle junior became the new tenant. He proved to be a very up-to-date and expert potter, as well as a good business man, and took on a record number of 18 pupils prior to 1756 when he was made Governor of Newgate Prison in Bristol. William Taylor, who had worked at the pottery since the time of Frances Ward, then took over and in 1767 he married Susannah Stevens, the then owner of the Temple Back Pottery, remaining as head potter until the end of the century.

Meanwhile, in 1777 Richard Frank had given up his Redcliff pottery to take charge at Temple Back, and there he stayed until his death in 1785. His place was then taken by his son-in-law, Joseph Ring, who quickly closed down his distilling busi-

ness next door and extended the pottery. Up until that time Temple Back had been one of several enterprises in Bristol producing tin-glazed earthenware, but in 1786 Joseph Ring began making creamware, a considerably more refined product developed in Staffordshire, and was soon advertising as 'the only manufacturer of Queen's ware'. This enabled the pottery to flourish and keep up with the demands of an increasingly sophisticated public. Unfortunately, Ring was accidentally killed in 1788 'by the falling in of a warehouse', and the following year his wife Elizabeth took William Taylor into partnership, the new concern being titled Ring, Taylor & Company.

In 1792 the existing partnership was dissolved and Henry Carter and Joseph Ring's brother, Robert, both joined the firm, which was then retitled Ring, Taylor and Carter. Further changes quickly followed and between then and 1813 the Bristol Pottery, Temple Backs, traded variously as Ring & Carter (1793–97), Henry Carter (1798–1805) and finally Henry Carter & Company. In 1813 Carter, Elizabeth's son, Joseph

Underglaze painters at Pountneys' Fishpond Pottery, photographed in the late 1920s.

44

Ring junior, and the young John Decimus Pountney formed a short-lived partnership called Carter, Ring & Pountney, but following Ring's unforeseen death the same year the company became Carter & Pountney, an arrangement that lasted until 1816. In that year the invalid Henry Carter finally retired and Pountney, together with Edwin Allies, entered into partnership to carry on the work of manufacturing 'printed, painted, enamelled and cream coloured earthenware'.

To consolidate his position, in 1821 J.D. Pountney acquired all of the freehold and lease-hold properties that made up the pottery prem-ises, together with its fixtures and implements, and it was under his direction that the Bristol Pottery entered into a period of great prosperity. As well as being a successful industrialist, Pountney also found time to undertake public duties, not only becoming president of both the Gloucestershire and Dolphin Societies, vice-pres-ident of the Chamber of Commerce, a councillor and alderman, but also serving as Mayor of Bristol in 1847.

The Pountney & Allies period at the Bristol Pottery continued until the junior partner's retirement in 1835, but the following year he was replaced by Gabriel Goldney, an existing company employee, the new Pountney & Goldney phase lasting through to 1849 when the latter left to become a traveller for Messrs. Finzell & Company, the sugar refiners. Pountney then carried on alone, trading as J.D. Pountney until, in December 1852, at the age of 63, he collapsed after supervis-ing the firing of a kiln and died a few hours later in his manager's house. His widow, Charlotte, then took control of the company, to which she devoted herself for the next 20 years. Between 1854 and 1857 the firm was known as J.D. Pountney & Company, and this was followed in 1858 by the brief partnership of Pountney, Edwards & Company, after which its name changed to Pountney & Company.

In 1865 the Bristol Pottery was advertised as producing 'all kinds of blue and white earthen-ware, in toilet, dinner, and tea ware, of which a large assortment is always kept in stock. Initials and crests printed to order. Samples may be seen at the works. A large assortment of china always kept on hand. Cheap vases in every variety and other ornaments, in Parian, etc. Pountney & Company, being appointed agents of some of the largest manufacturers of these goods, are able to supply them on most reasonable terms. This is the only blue & white earthenware manufactory within 90 miles of Bristol.'

After Charlotte Pountney's death in 1872 the Bristol Pottery was taken over for a short time by Captain Halsted Cobden, but in 1878 he sold out to Patrick Johnston and a Mr Rogers, two London solicitors, the former purchasing the latter's share upon his retirement in 1883. The following year Johnson died, by which time the business, which had not been enjoying good times, was on the verge of bankruptcy. This ailing company was then inherited by Thomas Bertram Johnston, a nephew of Patrick Johnston, who had worked at the pottery since 1882. It was he who made the decision to sell the Temple Back pottery and move to the Victoria Pottery, which has just come onto the market. The new premises, built in 1865 on Saint Philip's Marsh just behind Temple Meads station, proved to be suitable and the Bristol Pottery transferred there in 1886, by which time Johnston had paid off his debts and put the firm back on the road to recovery.

In 1889 Pountney & Company Ltd. was formed with Johnston and Charles Burns, a former com-pany clerk, as joint managing directors, after which the newest machinery was introduced to replace hand work and the pottery brought up to date. Nevertheless, during the last decade of the 19th century Johnson came to the conclusion that the company's future lay in building an up-to-date works elsewhere, and in 1900 Heward Bell, a man who possessed the necessary capital, was per-suaded to join the Board of Directors.

Soon afterwards an eight-acre site was acquired in Lodge Causeway, Fishponds, and here was laid out a new single-storey factory, complete with raked roofs and skylights and a line of beehive kilns running down the centre. Its design was rev-olutionary, turning raw material fed in at one end

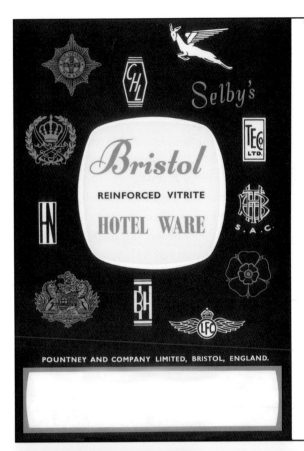

into finished articles that emerged from the other, while the new building provided a relatively healthy environment with light, well-ventilated workrooms. The premises, which were conveniently situated near to a main road, Fishponds railway station and the local coal mines, opened in April 1905, heralding the start of a new period of prosperity for the Bristol Pottery, during which some 700 people were employed there, half of whom were women.

Good industrial relations were high on T.D. Johnson's list of priorities, and he actively encour-

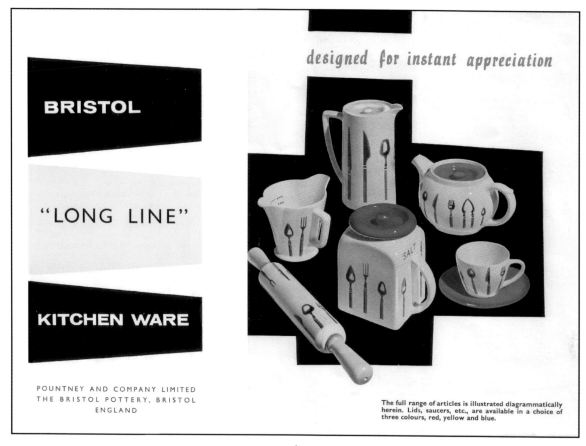

aged his workers to join trades unions, as well as providing them with welfare facilities, including a canteen, a sports ground and a social club. He also continued to take an active interest in the technical side of the business, and it was Johnson who ordered the first two continuously-fired ovens only months before his death in 1938. He left the firm in the hands of his son, Patrick Bertram Gwinnell Johnston, and his nephew, Alick Newsom, who became joint managing directors along with Arthur Adams, who had been previously employed as the pottery's commercial manager.

In 1950 William Cottrell replaced Adams as company secretary and joint managing director, while the installation of another electric tunnel kiln in 1953 and an oil-fired biscuit kiln in 1957 completed the company's transition from bottle ovens. By the beginning of the 1960s the three joint managing directors were approaching retirement, but as no family members were available to follow them Christopher Clifford from the Royal Worcester factory was appointed to Pountneys'

Board, and by 1963 he was acting as the chairman and sole managing director.

Unfortunately, the company he headed had several serious problems as not only was it facing increased competition from rival firms in Stoke-on-Trent but it also found recruitment difficult as jobs in Bristol's engineering, packaging, confectionery and tobacco industries were all better paid. Clifford made sweeping changes in an effort to bring the Bristol Pottery up to date, but the huge factory was just too old and inflexible to survive in an increasingly competitive industry. Consequently, in 1968, in order to repay large debts, the Board agreed to sell the factory site and to relocate to a trading estate at Pool, between Camborne and Redruth in Cornwall, where labour was plentiful and wages were low. Closure finally came in the autumn of 1969, bringing an end to a continuous tradition of pottery in Bristol, which went back for well over 300 years.

The Fishponds site was subsequently sold to MacKenzie Hill Investments, and in December 1969 the unwanted plant and machinery was auc-

tioned off prior to the demolition of the buildings and the clearing of the site, on which now stands an industrial estate. In Cornwall the new factory opened in November 1969, at which time the firm's name was changed to the Cauldon Bristol Pottery, reflecting the fact that the Bristol company had purchased the name and goodwill of Royal Cauldon back in 1962. However, for a variety of reasons the venture failed, and in 1971 the firm went into liquidation, only to be purchased by A.G. Richardson of Stoke-on-Trent, makers of Crown Ducal Ware. Production in Cornwall finally ceased in 1977 when the business, which in 1983 became part of the Perkes Ceramics Group, was transferred to Ferrybridge, West Yorkshire, where Cauldon Potteries Ltd still operates today.

Bricks and Tiles

For many years Bristol was also a regionally significant producer of redware, such as bricks, pantiles, chimney pots, drain pipes, ornamental gar-

den pots, vases and fountains, the local brick and tile works and potteries producing these items taking full advantage of the vast amounts of locally occurring coal measures clay. By 1900 there were still about 19 brick works in operation within greater Bristol, with an equal number north and south of the River Avon, one of which was the Fishponds & Bedminster Brick & Tile Company, the owners of a 10-acre site at Fishponds. However, its life was relatively short and, although clay extraction began about 1880, in 1908 the firm went into liquidation, after which the old clay pit filled with water and subsequently became famous locally as the Alcove Lido. Today housing development has reduced the area of water dramatically and the only surviving building on the site is the company's old office in Ridgeway Road, which has been converted into a private dwelling.

This process of contraction within the local brick and tile industry was by no means confined to one company, and, in fact, was so rapid during the early 20th century that by 1920 the number of such firms had reduced to eight. Unfortunately, this trend continued and A.J. Bridges of Court Road, Kingswood, closed in 1926, followed by the Bristol Brick & Tile Company at Crofts End, St George, in 1934. This left just the Hollybrook Brick Company Ltd working at Chester Park, Fishponds, and Vale Lane, Bedminster; G.E & A.E. Fussel at Crofts End; the Ashton Vale Iron Company and John Prater & Company, both in South Liberty Lane, Bedminster and Scourse & Kingston nearby in

W. MEREWEATHER & CO.,

SOUTH BRISTOL

Brick and Tile Works,

PARSON STREET, BEDMINSTER,

BRISTOL.

OFFICE:—

South View House, West Street, Bedminster.

Clay extraction at the Ridgeway Road, Fishponds pit, operated by the Fishponds & Bedminster Brick & Tile Company, at the end of the 19th century.

The old offices of the Fishponds & Bedminster Brick & Tile Company at Ridgeway Road, Fishponds. This building still survives as a result of having been converted into a private house.

Parson Street, manufacturers of dry-pressed, white-glazed facing bricks.

Of these, the most famous was probably the Hollybrook Brick Company, already well established by 1882, which for many years was owned principally by the May family of Bath. On a site at Chester Park, bounded by Argyle Road, Whitefield Road, Duncombe Lane and Charlton Road, they manufactured wire cut common bricks as well as a salt-glazed facing brick, with the trade name of 'Hollychrome', while at Vale Lane a yellow, dry-pressed common brick was produced, something suitable only for use in internal walls. Hollybrook also operated two other works just outside Bristol, one being situated near the railway station at Warmley where the gritty local clay was used to make salt-glazed sanitary pipes and fittings. The other was at Westerleigh Road, Yate, where the introduction of manganese into the clay enabled engineering and facing bricks to be produced in a variety of colours, including red, brown, brindle and blue.

In about 1935 Hollybrook was taken over by Morgan Brothers & Company, a London based firm of accountants, at which time the chairman, Thomas Hughes Delabere May, JP, his two sons and Percival Seaton Jones, the managing director and company secretary, all retired. A new Board of Directors was installed, and by 1936 the firm had been renamed the Hollychrome Brick & Tile Company Ltd. During the early 1940s the Yate works was shut down and, with the clay reserves running out, the Fishponds site closed in around 1954, after which the clay-pit was sold to Bristol City Council, which filled it with household waste and grassed it over. The company's Vale Lane site did not survive much longer and work there finally came to an end in the early 1960s. This left just Warmley, which was sold in 1964 to the Hepworth Iron Company of Sheffield. This concern also acquired the rival Haskins Pottery, based nearby at Warmley Tower, and although that was closed in 1967 manufacturing continued on the old Hollychrome site until the 1970s.

Although brick making no longer takes place within the Bristol conurbation, such work is still carried on locally by Ibstock Brick Ltd who own the Cattybrook clay pit at Almondsbury, a few miles north of the city, as well as its satellite at Shortwood. The Cattybrook works in Over Lane was founded in 1865 by Charles Richardson, engineer of the Bristol & South Wales Union Railway, who had realised the potential of the local clay when the excavations were taking place for the nearby Patchway tunnel.

In 1871 he went into partnership with Ernest Street and Edward Grover, the business being incorporated in 1877 as the Cattybrook Brick Company Ltd, manufacturers of bricks and agricultural drainpipes. Over the years its high quality

The clay pit belonging to the Hollybrook Brick Works in Chester Park, photographed in 1965, about 10 years after brick making ceased.

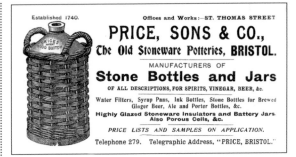

deep-red engineering bricks were used extensively by the construction industry in Bristol, while some 30 million of them went to line the 1872 Severn railway tunnel. Exactly 100 years later the company was purchased by Ibstock Johnsen Ltd, and in 1973 Cattybrooks' independent identity was lost when they were absorbed by Ibstock Building Products Ltd.

Stoneware

During the 18th century, salt-glazed stoneware began to be manufactured locally to satisfy the increasing demand for non-porous jars, jugs, mugs, and sugar moulds, and production continued until competition from North Staffordshire finally destroyed the industry. The most long-lived and famous of Bristol's stoneware potters was Price, Powell & Company, formed early in the 20th century by the amalgamation of Bristol's two largest manufacturers.

The firm claimed to have been established in 1740, although their origins in Temple Street are obscure, nevertheless Thomas Patience was working there as a stoneware potter as early as 1747, and by 1783 Joseph Reed & Company were employed as potters in premises nearby. In October 1785, two months before his death, Patience took Charles Price on as an apprentice,

and it was he, in about 1799, who became one of the partners in the firm of Price & Reed, established as 'brown stone potters', again in Temple Street. From then onwards the latter partner's name then began to be spelt as Read, and in around 1808 they also acquired James Alsop's old pottery in Thomas Street 'next to the Bunch of Grapes'. Between 1818 and 1822 Charles Price ran the firm alone, but from then until 1884 the company was variously known as Charles Price & Son (1823–42); Charles Price & Sons (1843–49); Charles & Joseph Read Price (1850–63), Joseph & Charles Price Bros. (1864–83) and Price, Sons & Company (1884–1906).

In 1853 Charles Price junior acquired Bright's Pottery in Temple Street, and by 1880, as manufacturers of the 'far famed Bristol stoneware, glazed inside and out with vitrified enamel', the firm was turning out a wide range of products. These included export jam, mustard, salt, spirit, pickling and preserve jars, screw or stoppered jars and jars cased in wickerworks, as well as ink, ginger beer, ale and porter bottles, cocoa pans, water filters, and 'every description of stoneware for domestic use' such as barrels and hot water bot-

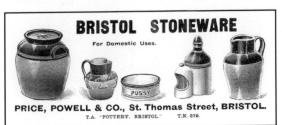

tles. Later, porous pots, cells, battery jars and insulators, for both industrial and domestic electrical applications, were added to the product range.

The other firm involved in the merger was William Powell & Sons, which had been founded about 1810 when William and Thomas Powell opened a 'Stourbridge Glass Warehouse' in Bath Parade, Temple Gate, where this broad glass used in windows was cut to the size required by the customers. Around 1816 they purchased a 'brown stone pottery' in Thomas Street, which was eventually relocated to the site of the defunct Red Lane glasshouse at Temple Gate, bought by the Powells in 1824. The company was known as William &

The fatal fire at Derham Brothers Boot Factory, St James Street, on 27 March 1906, which caused damage estimated at £60,000.

Thomas Powell up until 1831, then was briefly retitled William & John Powell, before William Powell took sole charge in 1833.

Up until this time the brown stoneware was salt-glazed, the salt being thrown into the kiln where it fell in a vaporised state upon the articles being fired. However, the procedure did not always work properly, prompting William Powell to develop, among other things, a glaze impervious to the action of any liquid with which it was likely to come into contact. In February 1835 the first lot of the new 'improved' ware was despatched from Temple Gate and his innovations were later introduced across the country. William Powell carried on the business alone until his death in 1854, after which his two sons took over, the firm then being known as William Powell & Sons. Finally, in 1907, Price, Sons & Company merged with William Powell and Sons to form Price, Powell & Company, by which time the St Thomas Street potteries were producing 'foot warmers, air tight pots and all varieties of jars and bottles' in addition to their 'Tripoli' porous stone filters. Price, Powell & Company were the last of Bristol's stoneware potters, and they continued on until final closure in about 1962.

Bootmaking

Over the years a number of industries in and around Bristol were heavily involved in supplying the needs of the collieries and quarries, and one of these, the boot makers, carried on working in the Kingswood area for many years after the last local pits had closed and stone extraction had ceased.

From mediaeval times most places of any reasonable size could boast either a resident cordwainer to make the everyday footwear people needed or, at the very least, a cobbler to repair it. This reliance upon individual craftsmen working from their homes continued until the mid-17th century when army boots began to be produced on a larger scale in Northampton. Other towns eventually followed their lead, with wholesale shoe manufacturing being established in Stafford in 1767, Norwich in 1792 and finally Bristol in 1845, where the Derham brothers set up a small factory in Nelson Street.

The sons of a doctor from Wrington in Somerset, they had begun in a small way by making children's shoes in their own house, but after moving to Bristol they moved several times before settling in extensive premises in St James Street.

Another view of the burnt out premises of Derham Brothers.

Views of Derham Brothers factories built as replacements for the old St James Street premises.

During the early 1850s the company introduced a riveting system for sole attachment and soon a great demand had been created among colliers and agricultural workers for their cheap, heavy-riveted footwear, not only from Bristol and the West Country but also from South Wales. Consequently, by 1883 the company had up to

1,500 regular workers and a labour force that exceeded 2,000 at times of peak demand, making Derhams one of Bristol's largest employers. However, they were not alone, and six years later a local trade directory commented that 'the leather trade of Bristol is famed over the world and the manufacture of boots and shoes is surpassed by few towns.'

Attracted by the fact that it possessed natural advantages regarding both rail and sea communication and that they considered 'Bristol as the front door of England', in June 1898 Lennards, a firm founded in 1877 and incorporated in 1897, began transferring their business down to the Temple area of the city, a move which was completed the following year. The company operated from these temporary premises for three years until their magnificent new headquarters building in Queens Road, Clifton, was finally completed. Fed from their own Northampton works, by 1930 the Bristol distribution centre was responsible not only for supplying about 250 branches across the country but also the operation of a mail order service, which reached customers in some 70 countries. In 1938 the company moved its headquarters to Soundwell Road, Staple Hill, and by the mid-1960s Lennards were famous from Penzance to Carlisle as multiple retailers of high quality shoes imported from Italy, France and Belgium.

On the production side, Bristol's boot and shoe industry reached its peak in 1891, in which year some 129 undertakings employing a total of around 10,000 men, women and children were operating in the area. These were concentrated in two localities, the first of which was in and around the parishes of St Paul and St James in the central area of the city, where the emphasis was on lighter footwear. Here, as well as Derham Brothers of St James Street, were based such firms as Cridland & Rose, who made high grade women's and men's shoes in King Square, Hutchings & May of Portland Square, wholesale and export producers, and H. Steadman & Company Ltd. of 24 Castle Green, who manufactured not only boots and shoes but also leggings.

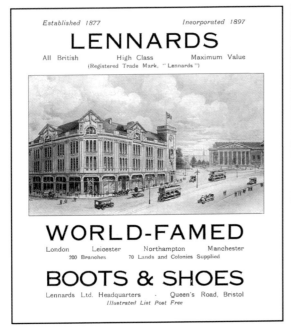
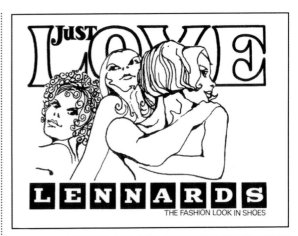

The other important sector of Bristol's boot and shoe industry was concentrated around Kingswood, where most firms specialised in the heavy duty part of the trade. Here local demand had encouraged a number of former miners and ex-employees of the larger makers to set up their own undertakings, spurred on by the fact that the amount of capital required was relatively small. In addition, as the technical expertise required to produce both industrial footwear and the popular high lace up ladies boots was not all that great, it was ideal work for those from other occupations.

Many of the factories relied heavily upon out workers who toiled away in cottage workshops all over the Kingswood area, and during the busiest season, which lasted from June through to December, it was not unusual for whole families to work through the night to maintain production. Although modern machinery began to be installed in local factories during the 1870s, hand work remained important and until the time of World War One outwork remained common around Kingswood. The first firms to set up in that locality had been J. Flook & Sons in 1847 and A. Fussell & Sons in 1855, the founder of the latter having himself worked as a collier who had begun making boots on a part-time basis. The local industry quickly grew, and by 1871 some 342 women and 276 men in Kingswood were working in the boot and shoe trade.

So successful was Fussells that 10 years later their Honey Hill factory was employing 400 people and nearby Albert Road, Wesley Road, Victoria Road and Regent Street had all been built by the company to house them. Meanwhile, in 1898 Dereham Bros. had become a limited liability company, and, following a disastrous fire, which in 1906 destroyed their St James Street premises, had relocated to a modern factory in Soundwell, right on the edge of Kingswood. In 1910 this was bought by Clifford and Percy Steadman of H. Steadman & Company, who made women's shoes in premises in Castle Green.

Among the other firms that have been based in Kingswood were Crates & Parker of Church Road and E.W. Pratt & Company of Park Road, an undertaking which for may years continued to manufacture the famous 'Holdfast' brand, while Hunt & Watts, established in 1887, occupied the Standard Boot Factory in nearby St George. Unfortunately, pay in the trade was generally low and the working day long, particularly during World War One when the demand for boots was at its peak. Then it was not unusual to work from 6am through until 7 or 8pm, with only a half-hour break being allowed for breakfast, an hour for lunch and half an hour in the afternoon.

It was the militancy of the workforce in central Bristol that had caused many of the large boot manufacturers in the city to expand in the Kingswood area, because here they were able to take advantage of a weak union and lower wages. Thus, by 1893 nearly all had set up branch factories in the locality. Up until that time the Kingswood undertakings had tended to be smaller than those in central Bristol, but this situation soon changed, the firm of G.B. Britton & Sons, which later attained national prominence, being probably the best example. The company can trace its origins back to 1880 when George Bryant Britton and George Jefferies set up in partnership and opened a factory in Waters Road, Kingswood, which was soon employing about 50 people.

In 1899 Jefferies retired and Britton built himself a new factory at Lodge Road, Kingswood, although he was slow to mechanise it, and by 1914

had some 150 out-workers. Nevertheles, industrial peace during the 1900s helped to make the early 20th century a prosperous time for many of the local footwear manufacturers, and in 1904 G.B. Britton entered into partnership with his two sons, George Ewart Britton and Samuel Wesley Britton. To keep up with demand, factory extensions were built by Britton & Sons in 1908 and 1914, by which time output was running at about 5,750 pairs of boots a week, while during World War One demand from the military ensured that Brittons' net profits tripled.

The 1920s, however, were difficult times, and with no service contracts, chronic high unemployment in mining and agriculture and the loss of important traditional markets following the creation of the new Irish Free State, the full effect of economic recession was soon felt by the local heavy footwear producers. This caused the industry to go into decline, and by 1931 there were only 71 footwear manufacturers left in the Bristol area. Meanwhile, in 1927, G.B. Britton's youngest son, Jack, had become a partner in the firm, only to take control of it in 1929 when his father died and to become its managing director when G.B. Britton & Sons Ltd was formed upon the retirement of his uncle, George Ewart Britton, in 1934. He guided the firm through World War Two when

again government contracts ensured the company's survival, while its insistence that Brittons find room for the machinery of F. Wiltshire & Company, one of its local competitors, led to the latter becoming a fully owned subsidiary of G.B. Britton & Sons Ltd in 1941.

During the early 1950s Somerset manufacturer C & J Clark Ltd developed reliable machines to carry out direct moulding, which involved a pair of rubber soles and heels being moulded, vulcanised and bonded to leather uppers in one process. However, as their expertise was limited to women's and children's shoes, in 1955 they agreed to supply machines to Brittons', who subsequently adapted them for boot manufacture. The new lines soon made them the dominant force in the local footwear industry,

Above: Hunt & Watts Standard Boot Factory in St George as it looked at the beginning of the 20th century.

Left: An interior photograph of E.W. Pratt & Company's 'Holdfast' boot factory in Park Road, Kingswood, taken during 1927.

Not surprisingly, supply was outstripping demand, and in order to increase production capacity Brittons' began taking over rival firms, Hoare & Douglas Ltd and Thomas Miles & Company Ltd, both in Kingswood, being absorbed in 1956 and 1959 respectively, while further acquisitions were made in 1959 in South Wales and Northern Ireland. This was followed in 1961 by the completion of a large extension at the Lodge Road factory and a successful take over bid for Wyles Brothers, a Midland multiple and wholesale concern. By this time production was running at between 10,000 to 50,000 pairs a week, mainly 'Tuf' boots and 'Gluv' shoes. David Wilcox replaced Jack Britton as managing director in 1963, and during the following years major overseas expansion also took place, with the establishment of manufacturing subsidiaries and distribution companies in a number of countries.

In 1968 Dereham Bros. Ltd, who had been producing medium-priced women's shoes, went into liquidation, and by the end of the decade only three firms were still in operation in the Bristol area, two small manufacturers in the city itself

the country's market leader in men's boots and shoes and its largest supplier of army and industrial safety footwear. The 'Everyday' shoe launched in 1959 was soon the biggest selling single line in the history of the industry, and such was Britton's growth that the total number of employees rose from 450 in 1951 to just over 3,000 in 1968, making it one of the top six footwear producers in Britain.

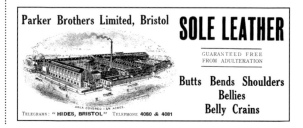

The empty Lodge Road premises of G.B. Britton & Sons, in 2002, shortly before demolition. A new housing development now covers the site.

A look inside Brittons' Lodge Road factory in 1968.

and the mighty G.B. Britton in Kingswood. However, that year saw Brittons' profits fall sharply, increasing competition from rival British firms and cheap foreign imports, plus complacency, which prevented the firm from introducing replacement products, all having conspired against Brittons.

As a consequence, the workforce was cut and David Wilcox replaced as managing director, but this could not prevent the firm's take over by the Northampton-based Ward White Group, and G.B. Britton & Sons Ltd became a wholly owned subsidiary of Ward White on 20 July 1973. Only the Kingswood and South Wales operations were retained, and by 1985 the workforce at Kingswood had fallen from 1,000 to 750, ensuring that the 'Tuf' brand prospered, while the company retained its position as a major producer of safety footwear and army boots. Production continued at Kingswood until 2001, by which time the factory, by then part of the UK Safety Group Ltd, employed just 130 people. Sadly the doors closed for the last time in December of that year, although the marketing operation moved to Yate where the firm continued to operate as a division of the UKS Group.

CHAPTER 4

Lead, Tin and Zinc

The Sheldon Bush & Patent Shot Company

The production and working of lead is something that was carried out in the Bristol area from pre-Roman times right up until 1994. For many centuries the mines on the Mendip Hills were the source of the lead used locally, and during the 1670s improvements to the reverberatory furnace enabled pit coal to be employed in the lead-smelting works at Bristol. Even after about 1850, when lead mining finally ceased on the Mendips, Cornish mining engineers moved in to successfully rework the vast quantities of slag that had accumulated over the centuries, an activity that continued until 1908.

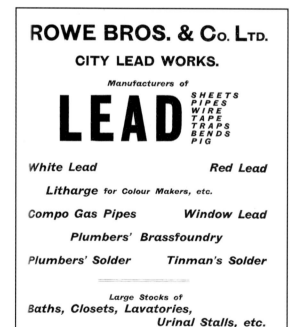

ROWE BROS. & Co. Ltd.

CITY LEAD WORKS.

Manufacturers of

LEAD

SHEETS
PIPES
WIRE
TAPE
TRAPS
BENDS
PIG

White Lead　　　　　*Red Lead*

Litharge for Colour Makers, etc.

Compo Gas Pipes　　*Window Lead*

Plumbers' Brassfoundry

Plumbers' Solder　　*Tinman's Solder*

Large Stocks of
Baths, Closets, Lavatories,
Urinal Stalls, etc.

CANONS' MARSH,
BRISTOL.

Although Mendip lead, with its high arsenic content, was hard and, therefore, unsuitable for rolling into sheets or to use for plumbing, it was ideal for the manufacture of shot and bullets, and over the years demand for these products grew.

The Redcliff Hill Shot Tower, the world's first. Built in the 1780s and demolished for road widening in the autumn of 1968.

By the middle of the 18th century both bullets and shot were usually cast in moulds, but small shot was produced by dropping the molten lead into water and it tended to fall in globules rather than tears or strings. As a result, it was usually unevenly shaped, and had to be placed in a churn and rotated until friction produced something approaching a sphere. There had to be a better way, and it was William Watts, a Bristol plumber, who discovered that the answer lay in dropping the molten lead from a considerable height. In December 1782 he was granted his famous patent for 'Making small shot solid throughout, perfectly globular in form and without dimples, scratches and imperfections, which other shot thentofore manufactured usually had on their surface.'

resulting globules from being flattened on impact, was in proportion to the size of the shot required. To exploit his discovery, in January 1785 he took out a lease on an old house in Redcliff Hill where he cut a hole through the floors, deepened a well in the caves beneath and built a small roof tower, so as to give him a total drop of some 90 feet. In so doing, William Watts had constructed the world's first shot tower, and in order to develop the process, which is still in use today, in 1787 he took on a partner, Philip George of brewing fame. Success quickly followed, even moving a certain John Dix to turn his hand to poetry, a task for which he was obviously ill suited!

> *Mr Watts very soon a patent got*
> *So that very soon only himself could make Patent Shot;*
> *And King George and his son declar'd that they'd not*
> *Shoot with anything else and they ordered a lot.*

Watts's innovation gave Bristol a near monopoly of lead-shot production in Britain, but although it soon provided him with a considerable fortune an unwise investment in a speculative building venture in Clifton caused him to be declared bankrupt in 1794. This left his partners, Philip George and Samuel Worrall, who subsequently purchased Watts's patent, to continue and expand Watts, George & Company, which by 1800 had been retitled Philip George & Patent Shot Company. To consolidate his metal interests, George also acquired shares in certain Cornish lead mines. The undertaking later became Messrs Christopher George & Patent Shot Company in 1818 and James Williams & Patent Shot Company in 1848, before, in 1863, it was finally taken over and renamed the Sheldon Bush & Patent Shot Company. This concern also had a sheet and pipe works in Cheese Lane and went on to operate the old Blackswarth lead works, where by the 1880s ores from Wales, the Isle of Man and Australia were being smelted and silver extracted as a by-product.

Just how he came to invent the new process has become the stuff of legend, and this would have us believe that inspiration came during a dream he had one night after falling asleep at the foot of the tower of St Mary Redcliff Church following a heavy drinking session. To add to the mystery there are two distinct versions of this tale. In the first it is said he imagined that the church was on fire and that as the lead on the roof melted it dropped to the ground, only to land in pools of water where it solidified as perfectly spherical shot. The alternative is that he dreamed that his wife was pouring molten lead on him from the tower of the church through the holes in a rusty frying pan.

Whatever his inspiration, Watts soon discovered that if he poured molten lead through a perforated zinc tray, the height between it and the vat of cold water placed beneath, to prevent the

During the mid-1860s the Royal Commission

A look inside Rowe Bros. City Lead Works at Canon's Marsh. During the late 1990s it was converted into part of the new 'Wildscreen World'.

on the Employment of Children undertook some investigations locally and these included inspecting the firm's premises at both Redcliff Hill and Cheese Lane, accompanied by Thomas Sheldon. He was able to inform the visitors that the hours worked were 6am to 6pm, although longer hours were sometimes necessary in August and September when there was a great demand for lead shot because of the shooting season. He went on to say that he disliked employing boys under the age of 11 or those who could not read or write.

Astonishingly, the old shot tower on Redcliff Hill survived until 1968, when Bristol City Council demolished it for road widening, a new 140 feet high replacement concrete tower having been opened that year in Cheese Lane. Production of lead shot at the new premises continued until 1994, but, after a period of standing derelict, in late 2002 the tower was sold by its then owners, Persimmon Homes, to Bristol based Hyland Properties who plan to incorporate the Grade II listed building into a high-tech office complex.

John Hare & Company

Over the years a number of Bristol firms have been involved in making paint, a process that originally made extensive use of local lead, and one of the earliest to be established was an undertaking which in later years became John Hare & Company (colours) Ltd, probably best remembered today for their 'Anchor', 'Rai-Lac', 'Rainbow', and 'Longard' range of paints.

However, for much of its existence the company competed with local rivals, both large and small, notably John Hall, founded in 1788 as glaziers, which produced its famous 'Brolac' and 'Murac' ranges first at premises in Broadmead and St Philip's Marsh and after World War Two at Hengrove and James Rudman Ltd, established in 1872, whose paints and varnishes were formulated in the Cambrian Color Works in River Street, near the Frome Bridge. Also active in this field were Rowe Brothers & Company of Canon's Marsh, white and red lead manufacturers, who described their 'Duresco' as 'the king of water paints'; Oliver Pragnell & Company Ltd of Broadmead, who made enamel paint and varnish, and Samuel Wills & Company, established in 1812, a concern previously known as Hellier & Wills, which operated the Castle Green Colour Works, responsible for the production of 'Audax' Chinese Lacquer, 'Kastelac' synthetic enamel, 'Wallpax' oil flat wax paint and 'Wills White Japan'. Neither should we forget A. Ireland's works in St Philip's, which specialised in 'Bright Venetian Red' and 'Glossy Black' paints.

CASTLE GREEN WORKS, BRISTOL.

The origins of what became John Hare & Company (Colours) Ltd can in fact be traced back to a young man born in Taunton in 1753, who was one of many from Bristol's hinterland to have flocked to the city during the 18th century to seek their fortunes. There at Temple Gate, close to Bath Bridge, John Hare senior established Hare's Colour Works, an enterprise that quickly became

a great success. In 1820 the firm passed into the hands of his sons, Charles Hare and Sir John Hare, and in 1840 to the next generation, the brothers Charles, John and Sholto Vere Hare. Charles died in 1855 and by the early 1880s the company, by then a prosperous and expanding business, was being run by three of the founder's descendants, Charles Bowles, Henry Grace and C. Felce Hare.

At that time the undertaking, which employed between 300 and 400 people, consisted of petroleum cellars in Arno's Vale; the Albert floorcloth factory and flax mills in St Phillip's Marsh, which had been purchased in 1862; the white lead works

and rolling mills in Avon Street, St Philip's, bought in 1848 from T.H. & H. Riddle; the oil and colour works at Bath Bridge and the Head Office and Floorcloth Works opposite Temple Meads station. In addition, John Hare & Company also had an oil and colour branch in London.

Hare's Colour Works, Temple Gate, in the early Victorian period. The truncated spire of St Mary Redcliff Church can be seen in the background.

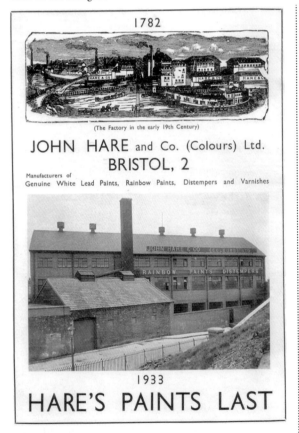

Like many other local businessmen, members of the Hare family also took an active part in the civic and public life of Bristol, and John Hare himself put considerable time and energy into the propagation of Nonconformism, his lasting legacy being the Zion Congregational Chapel in Bedminster, which opened in June 1830 and which was paid for entirely out of his own pocket. Likewise, Alderman Charles Bowles Hare

JOHN HARE & CO.,
(COLOURS), LTD.

Paint & Varnish Manufacturers

BRISTOL

The News Theatre, Peter Street, Bristol.

P. & A. Campbell's Pleasure Steamer.

A few illustrations of various types on which **HARE'S PRODUCTS** *were used.*

Hare's Paints and Varnishes famous for over 150 years.

Greyhound Racing and Speedway Track, Knowle Stadium, Bristol.

Grand Pier, Weston-super-Mare.

Bristol General Hospital.

Bench Hill Estate, Wythenshaw, Manchester.

Modern House, Frinton Park Estate, Frinton-on-Sea.

(1841–1911), son of Charles Bowles Hare of Clifton, at various times served as Sheriff of Bristol, Master of the Merchant Venturers, President of the Colston Parent Society, as a Justice of the Peace and Churchwarden of Redcilff parish, as well as involving himself in local musical, educational and charitable activities.

Although over the years the family's involvement with the firm lessened, under the name of John Hare & Co, (Colours) Ltd. it continued to manufacture paint at its Avon Street premises until about 1973, although some years before they had closed down the linoleum and floorcloth side of the business.

Capper Pass & Son Ltd

Since its foundation early in the 19th century, the firm of Capper Pass, which for many years was

A stylised drawing of young Capper Pass at his furnace.

forces into a shrinking labour market resulted in a steep rise in theft. One easy target for the gangs of criminals was non-ferrous metal and soon such things as brass door handles and knockers and lead roof flashing were disappearing from buildings all over Bristol.

Scrap metal dealers were the obvious receivers and following a tip-off the authorities raided Capper Pass's premises, where he was caught with over 1,200 pounds of stolen copper, worth some £75. At the subsequent trial, members of his workforce described the daily smelting of 1½cwts of metal, the majority of it stolen, and, as a result, in January 1819 he was found guilty of handling stolen metal. As the judge sentenced him to be transported for 14 years, Capper soon found himself aboard the 'Canada' en-route for New South Wales, where in 1828, as a 47-year-old ticket of leave convict conducting the business of tallow chandler in George Street, Sydney, he married Frances Johnson, a fellow transportee. Capper was back in court again in 1836 in a dispute over a horse, and although the following year his wife died he did not remain a widower for very long as in 1838 he married Anne Rose, again in Sydney.

In spite of the absence of the firm's founder, back in Bristol the family continued running the business and from unpromising beginnings a thriving concern soon began to emerge. In fact, the company became such a large concern that by the end of the 19th century the name of Capper Pass was well respected throughout Bristol, not only as enlightened employers but also as benefactors to the city.

One man in particular was responsible for this and that was Alfred Capper Pass, who was born in July 1837 in the small house in Avon Street where Capper Pass junior, his father, had been busy expanding the metal refining and dealing business. He was so successful that in 1840 the firm was able to relocate to larger premises in Paul Street a continuation of Mill Street, in Bedminster, close to an abundant supply of cheap coal. By 1850 the firm was employing six people, and during the following decades Capper Pass were processing gold and silver as well as lead and

involved with the recovery and refining of scrap or secondary metals, provides a tangible link between the old 18th century copper and zinc smelting industries and those of modern times. Capper Pass, who was from a family of Huguenot origin, was born in Walsall in Staffordshire in about 1781, and here he set up in business as a victullar, before marrying Ann Perkins in 1802. He then moved to Birmingham where he established himself as a 'refiner of metals and brass caster in general'. His son, Capper Pass junior, was born there in 1808 before the family again relocated, this time to Bristol, where they arrived sometime after 1812.

Here Capper began dealing in scrap metal, refining it at premises near the old gas works in Avon Street in St Philip's Marsh. This coincided with the end of the Napoleonic War, a time when the mass demobilisation of men from the armed

An aerial view of the Bedminster works of Capper Pass.

Part of the Capper Pass Workforce in the late 19th century.

copper. As they prospered the family moved to Richmond Road (now Cotswold Road), the first street to be built on Windmill Hill, and later over to Redland.

In 1866 the firm was retitled Capper Pass & Son, and in September of that year the first batch of tin alloy, or solder, was produced, while Alfred Capper Pass took control of the business following the death of his father in 1870. He was soon running it in a benevolently paternal way, ensuring that at Christmas his employees all got new shirts and their families presents. Alfred also assisted in times of hardship and during the winter gave his older workers warm woollen clothing, while supplying others with coal to allow them to dry out their houses when the local Malago stream overflowed. Workers housing was also made available up on Windmill Hill where he purchased the land, upon which was built St Michael and All Angels church.

Although Alfred Capper Pass expected great loyalty from his employees, their hot and dirty work was well rewarded as his firm paid wages

higher than the nearby iron foundry and even Fry's cocoa works. Like a number of other successful Victorian entrepreneurs, Alfred Capper Pass saw himself as something of an intellectual, and after becoming fascinated by the Roman artefacts he discovered during the course of resmelting lead slag from the Mendips he became a long term benefactor to the new University College establishing itself in Bristol. Here his name lives on, and in today's Department of Organic Chemistry there is still an Alfred Capper Pass Professorship.

During the latter part of the 19th century the Capper Pass concern became almost entirely involved in the manufacture of tin alloy, and between 1875 and 1882 the size of the factory doubled. Alfred also took into partnership his brother-in-law, Alfred Trapnell, before in 1894 the firm became a limited company, trading as Capper Pass & Son Ltd. Unfortunately, Alfred was in poor health by 1905 and, before his death in October, Stanley Baddock, a distant relation, was appointed company chairman.

Like many other manufacturers, during World War One the company prospered and throughout the 1920s continued refining high quality tin. However, as there was no convenient space available for expansion locally, in 1928 a new factory was established up at Melton in Yorkshire, just to the west of Hull. Here there was to be found a spacious level site with good rail access to the nearby port and adequate supplies of coal. It was also in close proximity to the Humber Estuary, from where cooling water could easily be obtained while abandoned clay pits were available nearby for dumping waste material.

Consequently, by the end of World War Two most workers had transferred north and in 1963 production ceased at the Capper Pass & Son plant in Bedminster, the company subsequently selling off the site for development. In comparison to Bristol, the Yorkshire works had a short life, its fate finally being sealed in 1985 when the relative price stability maintained by the International Tin Council collapsed in the face of new low cost production in Brazil. Faced with this, as well as the proliferation of processing plants in Third World producer countries, in 1991 Rio Tinto Zinc, its owners since 1967, were forced to close Britain's only tin smelter. Its legacy, however, lives on, and the company are still embroiled in bitter litigation over the health of many ex-employees of Capper Pass's Melton plant.

The Imperial Smelting Corporation

In 1905 a group of Melbourne business men set up the Zinc Corporation Ltd in order to process lead and zinc residues from the famous Broken Hill ore field in New South Wales. Germany soon obtained the contract to process the zinc concentrates which, after refining, Britain imported as commercial metallic zinc, a substance also known as spelter. With the outbreak of war in 1914 the whole situation changed, and with Britain left only with the alternative of obtaining zinc from the US, the Australians cancelled the German contracts.

The raw material was then offered for sale on a long term basis to any smelting plant that might be built in the UK, and government initiatives soon led to the formation of the National Smelting Company. After examining a number of locations close to ports, the decision was taken to

The Imperial Smelting Corporation's Avonmouth plant.

build the smelting works at Avonmouth, along with a plant for the production of sulphuric acid that was required by the Ministry of Munitions. A 400-acre site near the Royal Edward Dock, and conveniently adjoining the St Andrew's Road Railway Station, was purchased from Philip Napier Miles, owner of the King's Weston estate, and between 1917 and 1923 the new smelter was erected at a cost of over £800,000.

Unfortunately, after the war demand for zinc plummeted, and the National Smelting Company ran into difficulties before being rescued by a team of eminent British industrialists with interests in metals and chemicals. Having been placed back on its feet, in 1929 the company passed into the hands of the newly formed Imperial Smelting Corporation Ltd. Over the years the technology on the site progressed from the early Horizontal Retort and Vertical Retort processes to the development of the so called 'Imperial Smelting Process' and, following its operation on a pilot scale, the process went on to be licensed world-

An aerial view of the new Avonmouth Zinc Smelter shortly after it was opened in 1923.

An aerial view of Imperial Smelting Corporation's Avonmouth plant in the late 20th century.

wide, quickly becoming a major contributor to the world of zinc and lead production.

In 1949 the Imperial Smelting Corporation Ltd combined with the Zinc Corporation Ltd to become the Consolidated Zinc Corporation Ltd, or Conzinc, with its headquarters in London, and this in turn merged with Rio Tinto in 1962. During 1967 and 1968 extensive redevelopment took place at the Avonmouth smelter, making it the world's largest, and the £14 million blast furnace complex, which of course used the 'Imperial' process, was, with certain upgrades and improvements, to last until the plant finally ceased operating. Further changes came in 1971 when, seeking further control over downstream processing, the

Zinc Corporation and the British New Broken Hill Consolidated, then owned one third by CRA, merged to become Australian Mining and Smelting.

CRA came to be responsible for the operation of the Avonmouth smelter, not only the sole primary zinc producer in Britain but, by way of its by-products, also a large scale manufacturer of lead bullion, cadmium and sulphuric acid. Unfortunately, back in 1969, many workers were diagnosed as suffering from lead poisoning and a government enquiry was held into the plant's operations. Three years later Duncan Dewdney, RTZ's chief executive in Britain, 'openly confessed that, the plant's initial construction was skimped, that corners were cut and that it should have cost at least two million pounds more', and, as a result, extensive modifications had to be put in hand.

This was not a good time for Commonwealth Smelters, who suffered so many problems during the 1970s that in 1983 a survival plan had to be pushed through, and this resulted in the workforce being reduced from 1,000 down to around 700. As a result, profits soon rose, and although further setbacks were experienced in 1985, by the end of the decade Avonmouth was a comparative economic success story. Meanwhile, in 1988 Pasimco had been formed by the merger of the zinc-lead-silver mining, smelting, and international marketing activities of CRA and NBH, and in late 1993 it sold its British based operations to MIM Holdings, an Australian based mining and mineral processing company.

At the Avonmouth plant, which they renamed Britannia Zinc Ltd, the company continued with the manufacture of the various grades and qualities of zinc required by the galvanising, brass making, die casting, dust and oxide industries, which were subsequently transformed into products for the construction, automotive, and consumer durable market. However, times were changing, and as such customers such as the car industry, which for many years used zinc for dash boards, door handles and many other components, switched over to using plastic so the demand for the metal fell. This loss of market, coupled with low world prices and a high pound, forced MIM Holdings to announce the closure of Britannia Metals, with production of zinc and sulphuric acid finally ending during the last week of February 2003.

The Origins of Soapmaking

Of all the activities that Bristolians have engaged in over the years, one of the first to be established that made full use of the abundant supply of locally available coal was soap making, a precursor of today's massive chemical industry. Bristol was said to have been the first city in England to have made soap, London not having started production until the early 16th century. Consequently, as early as 1180 it was reported that 'in Bristol there was no one who is not, nor was not, a soap boiler', while until soap making commenced in the capital it appears that much of the country was being supplied with 'gray sope from Bristol'.

The original product was by modern standards somewhat crude and, instead of being used by people during the course of their daily ablutions, was employed in the manufacture of woollen cloth. Nevertheless, by the mid-16th century not only were Bristol soap boilers importing Spanish olive oil, used to produce a better quality product suitable for personal cleansing, but they had also established the Company of Soap Makers, a local guild with its own hall in the city. Bristol's position as the country's major soap producer lasted through until 1632 when Charles I granted a monopoly to certain London producers.

This caused Bristol's allocation to be reduced to 600 tons per annum by 1637, while the number of manufactories in the city fell to just 11. During the next decade the local industry fragmented, so that by about 1650 there were probably between 40 and 50 individual manufacturers in Bristol. A number of these seem to have been located in the harbour area where important ingredients such as olive oil and the alkaline ashes of burnt plants were both landed.

In spite of this severe setback the Bristol soap-making industry did not become extinct, and although it expanded again during the 18th century it remained a predominantly small-scale affair until the removal of Soap Duty in 1853. Nevertheless, by that time two predecessors of what was to become Bristol's largest and longest surviving soap manufacturer had already been operating for over a hundred years. Of these, the oldest was Farrell, Vaughan & Company of Christmas Street, which was already in existence in 1743, at which time the partners were listed as being Joseph Farrell, John Vaughan, Joseph Fry and William Jones.

Christopher Thomas & Brothers Ltd

The other Samuel Fripp and Company claimed to have been established in 1745, its partners being Samuel Fripp and Henry Davis. In 1771 they amalgamated to form Fry, Fripp & Company, the

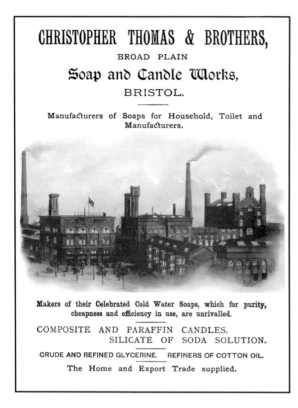

new firm being based in Castle Gate. The proprietors were all prominent in Bristol society, Farrell having been President of the Dolphin Society, a local charity, and Jones a Master of the Merchant Venturers, while Fry had his own chocolate business and both Vaughan and Davis were involved in banking. With such men at the helm it is not surprising that the firm prospered, and in 1783 the company acquired additional premises in Broad Plain, St Philips.

However, in 1787 Joseph Fry died, and, as by that time three of the five partners in the firm were members of the Fripp family, the concern became known as Samuel Fripp & Company. This trend for renaming continued regularly as various partners came and went, the title being William & James Fripp & Company between 1810 and 1819, then William Fripp & Company until 1827, after which the firm was known simply as Fripp & Company. During the 1820s and 1830s Bristol was the country's third largest manufacturing centre after London and Liverpool, and, although by 1825 there were some 24 soap and candle makers working in Bristol, of the 3,600 tons of soap produced annually in the city about half was made by

Fripp & Company. The business continued as a family concern until 1841 when it was decided that the best way forward was some form of merger with T. Thomas & C.J. Thomas, a more recently established firm of Bristol soap makers.

The Thomas family were originally from Llangadogg in Carmarthenshire, where Thomas traded as a wholesale grocer, butter merchant and haberdasher. His business dealings, however, often brought him to Bristol, where, in 1814, he began manufacturing soap at premises in Castle Street. Ten years later he entered into partnership with Stephen Thomas and his son-in-law, John Jones, both soapboilers, to form a company known as Jones, Thomas & Thomas, which was based at the Old Red Lion Yard in Redcliff Street. In 1831 the undertaking was renamed T. Thomas & C.J. Thomas when he brought into the firm his two sons, Thomas Thomas junior and Christopher James Thomas.

Ten years later Thomas Thomas senior retired, and in November 1841 Edward Bowles Fripp senior invited the Thomas brothers to form a partnership with his son, Edward Bowles Fripp junior. It was decided that the new firm was to be based at the Fripp's premises in Broad Plain, and although Thomas's family had produced tallow soap made from animal fat, whereas the Fripps had specialised in olive oil soap, both were subsequently manufactured by Thomas, Fripp & Thomas.

The last of the Fripp family to have any connection with the soap industry was Edward Bowles Fripp junior, and following his retirement in 1855 the company was renamed Christr. Thomas & Bros., to represent the partnership of Christopher, Thomas, Herbert, and Charles, which lasted until 1872 when Thomas died. Christopher's retirement followed in 1877, after which Charles, the youngest of the brothers, became the leading light in the business.

The years 1856 to 1889 can really be described as the company's 'golden era'. The abolition of Soap Duty and the scrapping of various regulations concerning the manufacturing of soap in 1853 had allowed innovative production tech-

niques to be introduced and modern plant of the type already in use abroad to be installed in the factory. Shortly after, the Crimean War caused supplies of Russian tallow to be cut off, initiating a gradual switch over to the use of palm kernel oil as the basic ingredient in many brands of soap.

To accommodate these changes the original 1841–3 buildings in Broad Plain were extended between 1865 and 1867 while, following a trip to Italy, Charles had the whole works practically rebuilt in the Bristol Byzantine style during 1882. The results certainly were impressive, and shortly after it opened an observer was moved to write 'In viewing the premises of this manufactory, one is struck with the unique chimney towering high above one of the principal additions to the other buildings. This is said to be an exact copy of the Tower of Palazzo Vecchio, the great Town Hall of Florence.'

During the second half of the 19th century the production of hard soap increased to accommodate the growing demand, and although the company concentrated most of its efforts on marketing in the south-west of England and South Wales, by the early 1880s Christr. Thomas & Bros. was also successfully selling its cheap Cold Water Soaps in the industrial towns of Lancashire and Yorkshire. Nevertheless, with many of the raw materials required in the production of soap now arriving in Britain through London or Liverpool, it was becoming increasingly difficult for the company to compete effectively with producers in those places, and after 1886 profits were in decline. This change in fortune, plus a desire by some members of the family to release some of their capital, undoubtedly led to the transformation of the firm into a limited private company in 1889, while in 1897 Christr. Thomas & Bros. Ltd was put into voluntary liquidation and a new company incorporated.

By this time it had become clear that one man in particular posed the greatest threat to the Bristol soap makers, and he was William Hesketh Lever of Lever Brothers, a wholesale grocer, who in 1885 had begun manufacturing his own 'Sunlight' soap brand. His mass-marketing tech-

An aerial view of Christopher Thomas & Brothers Broad Plain Soap Works.

competitors, and following a collapse in the profits of Christr. Thomas & Bros. Ltd the firm entered into negotiations with Port Sunlight. As a result, in 1912 the company passed from family ownership into the hands of Lever Brothers, who immediately began work on improving and extending the factory. During the 1920s and 30s all was well at Broad Plain, and with 'Sunlight' as the only real national brand, 'Puritan' soap was able to maintain a strong position in the south-west, some 5,000 tons a year still being produced in 1939.

Although by 1950 the Broad Plain operation was neither bankrupt nor inefficient, the industry was changing rapidly, and as Christr. Thomas & Bros. Ltd, with its limited factory area, was not manufacturing any soap or detergent powders, washing-up liquid or popular brands of toilet

niques and strong export trade soon established him as a force to be reckoned with, and by 1914 Lever Brothers were producing nearly a third of the country's soap at their Port Sunlight plant.

In 1898 Christr. Thomas & Bros. Ltd began, somewhat belatedly, to challenge the 'Sunlight' encroachment on its traditional markets by the introduction of a somewhat similar bland, olive-oil soap, sold under the name of 'Puritan' and supported by a large marketing campaign. However, while the Bristol factory turned out a wide variety of products, Lever devoted his huge production capacity to just a few, ensuring that his cost would always be lower and his profits higher. Consequently, by the end of the decade Lever Brothers alone were supplying 17 percent of the British soap market, while Christr. Thomas & Bros. Ltd's annual output of around 6,750 tons represented just 2 percent.

Nevertheless, the company did its best to meet the ever increasing challenge, and during the early part of the 20th century Charles Thomas's son, Herbert Russell Thomas, was able to preside over the replacement of steam by electricity in the Broad Plain factory. Modern cooling machines were also installed, while in 1905 the company acquired the other Bristol soap producer Lawson & Company and, after absorbing its brands, sold off its Marsh Soap Works in St Philips.

In 1907 Lever began a policy of acquiring his

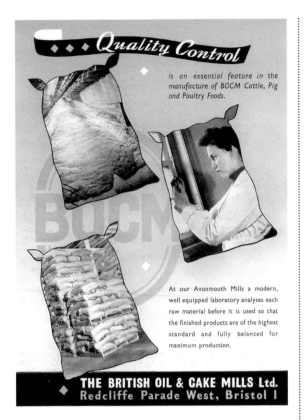

years had been used not only to make soap but also to manufacture candles and refine oil, tallow and glycerine. After the plant and machinery had been removed, in July 1954 the site passed into the hands of Moreland Investments & Property Ltd., and today much of the old Christopher Thomas works is occupied by the Gardiner Homecentre.

Christopher Thomas, the man who gave his name to the company, was Liberal in his politics and represented the St Philips ward between 1845 and 1887. He was also a member of Bristol City Council's Docks Committee from 1848 to 1878 and served as President of the Anchor Society in 1853 before becoming a JP the following year. In addition, Thomas involved himself in raising money for a number of good causes, including the Bristol General Hospital, while still finding enough time to attend meetings of the Bristol Chamber of Commerce and to act as chairman of the Bristol & South Wales Union Railway in 1863.

Along with other members of the family, both Christopher and Charles Thomas were noncon-formists, the two being deeply involved with the Unitarian Chapel in Lewins Mead and later in the development of the Oakfield Road Chapel at

soap, its future was in doubt. Consequently, on 14 April 1953, Unilever announced that the factory would shut, thereby closing a long chapter in the history of the Broad Plain works, which over the

Christopher Thomas & Brothers old Broad Plain works still survives today as the Gardiner Homecentre, operated by Gardiner Son & Co. Ltd.

Clifton. The Thomas' religious background accounted for the company's benevolently paternal treatment of their employees, who during the latter part of the 19th century were provided with benefits unheard of in most other local industries. These included not only free medical care, provided both in the factory as well as at home, a week's paid holiday, a summer outing and a 10 shilling bonus at Christmas but also medals for long service and a pension paid upon retirement. In 1881 the firm, which considered its workers to be part of one large family, was employing 193 men, about eight salesmen and 64 boys, the latter being dispatched each summer to farms in Somerset, where they were provided with a week's free holiday.

This comprehensive package helped to compensate for the 60-hour working week, and the fact that although key members of staff at Broad Plain were well paid, a foreman soap boiler receiving as much as £3 a week in 1870, others were less generously rewarded. Unusually, workers were called by their Christian names, and even after Lever Brothers had taken over their welfare remained an important consideration, a new sports ground being purchased at Hengrove Lane, Knowle, as late as July 1935. This caring attitude

continued until the factory finally closed, when the remaining employees were either transferred to other Unilever operations, such as the British Oil & Cake Mills, or offered much higher redundancy payments than were required by law.

Chemicals

By the end of the 18th century the foundations of today's multi-billion pound chemical industry had been well and truly laid, as modern, scientifically-based manufacturing processes began to be introduced into works across Britain. Locally, one early entrant into the field was H. & T. Proctor, who leased a site in Prewett Street from 1812 until 1966. Here, in a plant which incorporated a late 18th century glass cone, they made artificial fertilisers from materials such as bone, guano and nitrate of soda. By 1867 their Cathay Chemical Works was producing 'special manures' for turnips, mangols and potatoes, which Proctors considered as being, 'of superior quality and the most economical which are manufactured'. The factory's old glass cone remained a prominent local landmark until 1936 when a crack which had developed in its brickwork caused it to be reduced in height from 60 feet to about 25 feet. Fortunately, it still survives in this truncated form

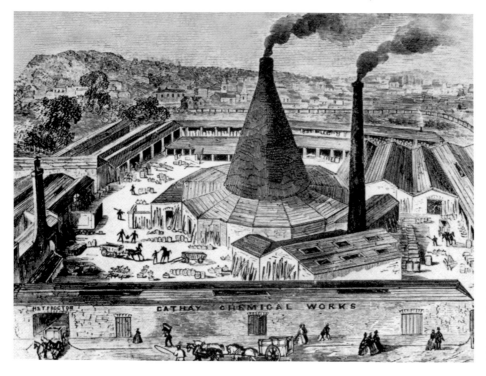

H. & T. Proctor's Cathay Chemical Works, which incorporated the old Redcliff glass cone.

An elevated view of H.&T. Proctor's chemical works as it appeared during the 1880s.

H.&T. Proctor's chemical works viewed from the railway line, which ran parallel with Redcliff Way.

as it was later transformed into the Glass Kiln Restaurant of the Hilton National Hotel in Redcliffe Way.

The first substances to be produced on a large scale were soda and vitriol, better known today as sulphuric acid, a substance which continued to be manufactured locally by ISC Chemicals until the early 21st century. However, the introduction of coal gas lighting into homes and factories during the early 19th century was really responsible for the consolidation of the chemical industry, as it immediately began to exploit the by-products of

The truncated Redcliff Glass Cone, the last surviving fragment of the Bristol's long extinct glass industry.

the gas production process. This created an ever increasing demand for more sophisticated chemical products, a need which for many years has been met by several important Severnside-based concerns. One of the best known of these is Philblack, Britain's leading producer of carbon black, a product used not only to colour rubber tyres but also as an ingredient in printing ink, paints and plastics.

The Netham Alkali Works

With its requirement for a reliable source of alkali, soap making was an activity heavily dependent on the fledging chemical industry, and so it is not surprising that the financially astute Charles Thomas should have made his largest personal investment in a local producer. This undertaking was the Netham Alkali Works and it had, like a number of other firms engaged in dirty, unpleasant and noxious trades, chosen to conduct its business some two miles east of the centre of Bristol, alongside the River Avon in the Crew's Hole valley.

The origins of what was to grow into a concern covering some 65 acres can be traced back to 1845 when Stephen Cox took over Henderson & Vesey's bankrupt Netham Works. He subsequently entered into partnership with a Mr Score, and in 1852 the pair established themselves as manufacturers of vitriol and alkali. Unfortunately, the business failed to flourish and, with the partnership dissolved, just seven years later Cox followed his predecessors into bankruptcy. The works was then taken over by its principal creditors, one of whom was Joseph Wethered, a leading local coal owner.

A Samuel Loxton drawing from 1913 showing the Netham Lock on the Feeder Canal. In the top left hand corner can be seen part of the Netham Alkali works.

At this time Charles Thomas, the soap manufacturer, also began investing heavily in the newly constituted firm, becoming one of the directors of Thomas, Prichard & Wethered Ltd as it was known before being officially registered as the Netham Chemical Company Ltd in August 1859. Expansion followed, and soon the company was producing not only sulphuric acid, caustic soda, soda crystals and bleaching powder, but also superphosphates for use as manure, and the ammonia-based chemicals used in galvanising, all derived from the liquor supplied by the Bristol Gas Company.

In 1861 Philip Worsley was appointed manager of the Netham Chemical Company Ltd, but was surprised to find that 'there was too much drinking and for want of a foreman checking their work the workmen often spoiled the materials for want of care and laziness, besides doing far less than a proper quantity for their day's work'. To combat the problem he 'gradually introduced improved methods and instituted a system of regular sampling and testing the various stages of the work'. Government investigators looking into the employment of children visited the works in 1866 and noted that at that time the Netham company employed some 200 men and 35 boys. Six of the boys were under 13 years of age, and one 10-year-old, who had been working there for about a year, toiled from 7am until 5pm breaking stones with a hammer, for which he received the princely sum of three shillings per week.

By the 1880s the firm had expanded to such an extent that its workforce numbered between 400 and 500 men, of which the lime dressers and bleach packers were by far the best paid, reflecting the dangers they faced from the deadly chlorine gas while handling these materials. In order to carry out such work for any length of time it was not only necessary for the operatives to wear goggles and three-inch thick masks made of dampened flannel wrappings but also to smear grease on their hands and arms!

Nevertheless, in an attempt to modernise production methods and to a certain extent reduce pollution and the malodorous outpourings from the site, the factory's plant was regularly upgraded, beginning in 1869 when a 300-feet high chimney was built. The great improvements made at Crew's Hole certainly did not go unrewarded, and in 1871 Worsley was made a director of the company. Although his career in industrial chemistry was his main preoccupation, he still found time to serve as chairman of the local St

George's School Board and vice-chairman of the new University College then being established in Bristol. During his lifetime Philip Worsley also gave the majority of his collection of books on chemistry to the fledgling university, where the Worsley Chemical Library was created in his honour.

In 1890 the Netham Chemical Company Ltd merged with several similar concerns, and Worsley was made a director of the newly constituted United Alkali Company Ltd. This remained an independent concern until 1929 when it merged with three other firms to form Imperial Chemical Industries Ltd. During the 1930s the plant turned out some 400 tons of soda per week, in addition to 1,000 tons of sulphuric acid, 1,000 tons of hydorchloric acid, 500 tons of saltcake, together with large quantities of ammonia compounds and other chemicals. Although much of the soda was supplied to the soap industry, it was also employed in glass and paper making as well as by textile manufacturers.

The sulphuric acid was used in electrical accumulators, for the production of fertilisers, dyes and explosives and by the tinplate and galvanising industries, which also took large quantities of hydrochloric acid. Saltcake, produced by the decomposing of common salt with sulphuric acid, was another product supplied to the glass makers, as well as being important in the manufacture of wood pulp. The Netham Chemical Works of the United Alkali Company Ltd remained part of the vast ICI empire until 1949 when the outdated plant was finally shut down. However, an ICI presence was soon re-established in the area when, in 1960, they began building a 1,000-acre petro-chemical complex at Severnside, which over the years has provided employment for many local people.

William Butler & Company

Another well known chemical firm that established itself in Crew's Hole was William Butler &

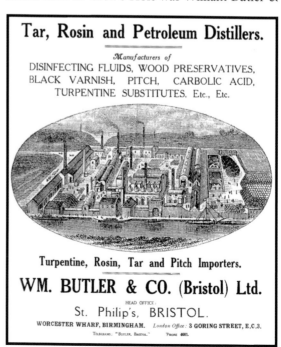

An aerial view of William Butler & Company's Crew's Hole Works, taken during the 1940s.

Company, which concerned itself with processing coal tar, the residue from gas production. One of the first by-products to find a commercial application was creosote oil, patented as a wood pre-

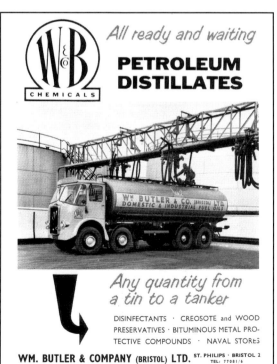

All ready and waiting

PETROLEUM DISTILLATES

Any quantity from a tin to a tanker

DISINFECTANTS · CREOSOTE and WOOD PRESERVATIVES · BITUMINOUS METAL PROTECTIVE COMPOUNDS · NAVAL STORES

WM. BUTLER & COMPANY (BRISTOL) LTD. ST. PHILIPS · BRISTOL 2 TEL: 77081/6

servative in 1838 by John Bethell of West Bromwich, and from whom Isambard Kingdom Brunel obtained a manufacturing licence in order to treat his wooden railway sleepers.

Roberts & Daines of Silverthorne Lane, St Philips, provided the capital for the tar distilling project, and in 1843 William Butler, a staunch Methodist who had worked with Brunel on the Bristol and Exeter Railway, came to Bristol to manage the concern, which he did successfully for the next 20 years. Unfortunately for Roberts and Daines, they suffered a fire so serious in 1863 that they decided to call it a day and sold the business to their manager, who continued to run it under the title of William Butler & Company. In the early years the only saleable product, other than creosote and lamp black, was pitch, which was mixed either with unusable coal dust to produce briquettes or with gravel to produce tarmacadam for surfacing roads.

This soon changed and Butlers' subsequent expansion led him to lease part of Roberts & Daines premises in Silverthorne Lane, which went on to become not only their railhead and storage depot but also the head office of what was becoming a very successful family concern. Premises were later acquired in Gloucester, which were served by river with six lighters and a steam tug, while the firm also owned four trows for the South Wales trade, as well as a coasting steamer. They even went on to acquire a manufacturing plant in the US.

During the second half of the 19th century, William Butler & Company busily expanded their product range of oil-based chemicals as new uses were discovered for the products of tar distillation. Thus benzene, anthhracine, napthalene, and phenol all found applications in the new artificial dye industry, while the latter was also used to prepare the carbolic acid solution used as an antiseptic in hospitals. The introduction of the motor car at the end of the 19th century led to the firm starting to separate motor benzole from the light distillate, and soon there was a steady demand for the 'Highly Rectified Spirit', which retailed at 10 pence a gallon.

Aside from tar distillation, Butler was particularly interested in transport, and was not only instrumental in the setting up of the Bristol Tramways Company but also acted as its first chairman. Consequently, when he was finally lowered into his grave in 1900 all the trams of Bristol remained stationary for one minute. William Butler & Company was left in the hands of his sons, William and Thomas, both of whom were pioneer motorists, William having the distinction of being the first person to register a motor vehicle in Bristol.

The early 20th century saw the company continue to prosper, and in 1905 it was registered as

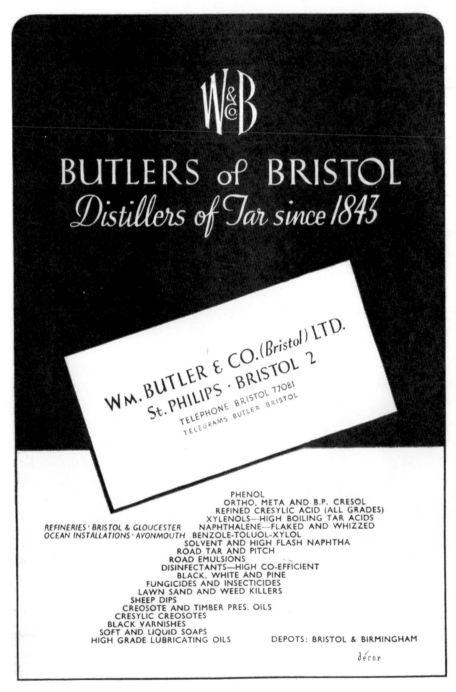

William Butler &
Company's Crew's
Hole Works, photo-
graphed in about
1972.

William Butler & Company (Bristol) Ltd. One reason for the firm's continuing good performance was the discovery of 'Bakelite', one of the first thermo-setting plastics, which ensured that phenol became in great demand after 1907. Likewise, toluene, used in the manufacture of explosives, was required in large quantities during World War One. Here, Butlers having the foresight to set up the first plant in the country for its production.

In 1935 Butlers became a public company, at which time interests were expanded to include a lubricating oil refinery, the importation and distribution of petroleum, rosin distillation and a naval store. During World War Two its products, including phenol, creosols, xylenols and high melting point tar acids, were used extensively in the preparation of plastics, synthetic resins, weed killers, disinfectants, aeroplane fuel and drugs,

although it was not until 1948 that Butlers restarted trading in petroleum products.

In 1947 the gas industry was nationalised and, following the negotiation of a long-term contract, the tar distilling side of the business was effectively separated from its other activities in January 1952 when the Bristol & West Tar Distillers Ltd. was formed. The new concern was owned 75 percent by William Butler & Company (Bristol) Ltd.

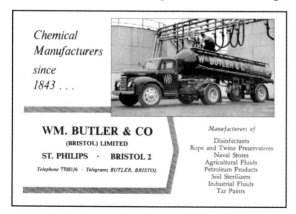

and 25 percent by the South West Gas Board. This arrangement lasted until 1962, when Butlers sold out their tar distilling interest to the Gas Board, and by 1965 they had transferred their remaining business to the new Rockingham Works at Avonmouth.

Here they operated as Butler Chemicals Ltd, and through its success a new company, Arndale,

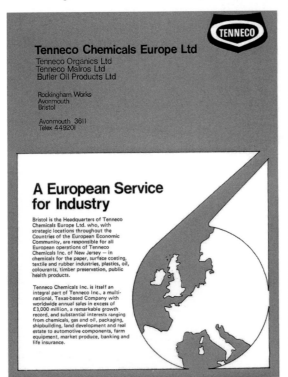

Tenneco Chemicals Europe Ltd
Tenneco Organics Ltd
Tenneco Malros Ltd
Butler Oil Products Ltd

Rockingham Works
Avonmouth
Bristol

Avonmouth 3611
Telex 449201

A European Service for Industry

Bristol is the Headquarters of Tenneco Chemicals Europe Ltd. who, with strategic locations throughout the Countries of the European Economic Community, are responsible for all European operations of Tenneco Chemicals Inc. of New Jersey — in chemicals for the paper, surface coating, textile and rubber industries, plastics, oil, colourants, timber preservation, public health products.

Tenneco Chemicals Inc. is itself an integral part of Tenneco Inc., a multinational, Texas-based Company with worldwide annual sales in excess of £3,000 million, a remarkable growth record, and substantial interests ranging from chemicals, gas and oil, packaging, shipbuilding, land development and real estate to automotive components, farm equipment, market produce, banking and life insurance.

owned jointly by Butler and the Belgian refiner Petrofina, was set up to act as a distributor for the chemicals. In 1972 the same partnership also established Butler Oil Products to handle petroleum sales and distribution, while in 1988 Petrofina purchased the balance of the shares in the Butler group. Finally, in 1998 the French company Total SA took over Petrofina to create the world's sixth largest oil group, and today Total Butler at Avonmouth, a subsidiary of TotalFinaElf UK Ltd, are one of the largest fuel oil distributors in the country.

By the end of the 1960s the phasing out of the traditional coal-based gas works had resulted in a considerable reduction in the availability of crude tar, and in 1970 the ownership of the Bristol & West Tar Distillers Ltd passed to the British Steel Corporation, Chemical Division, which in 1974 became British Steel Corporation (Chemicals) Ltd. It soon became obvious that the old Crew's Hole works was totally unsuitable for its purpose, and so in 1981 it was closed and the plant relocated to Avonmouth. Here, Tenneco Organics, a subsidiary of an American company, went on to produce disinfectants, antiseptics and preservatives, and continued to do so as part of Albright & Wilson, and finally Rhodia, the world's largest manufacturer of phosphate derivatives.

CHAPTER 6
Alcoholic Drinks

The Wine Trade

Of all the trades which grew up locally around the Port of Bristol, the oldest survivor, and one which over the years has done so much to make the name of the city famous, is that of wine importing. The origins of this trade can be traced back to 1152 when the Gascony region in south-west France passed into the hands of Henry Plantagenet, Count of Anjou, following his marriage to Eleanor of Aquitaine. Two years later he became King of England, thus opening the way for wine to be exported to this country, where insufficient domestic production ensured a ready market.

By the 13th century over 85 percent of all wine imported into England came from Gascony, and as it was shipped out through the port of Bordeaux, Bristol's position at the head of the Severn Estuary made it an ideal port of entry. Wine is first recorded as having been brought into the port in 1180, and by the beginning of the 14th century Bristol was importing some 756,000 gallons per annum. Although continental conflicts caused the trade to fluctuate over the years, Gascony continued to be the country's major source of wine until, by 1453, the whole of the region had been lost to the French.

Following this setback, the Bristol wine merchants increasingly turned their attention to alter-native sources in Spain and Portugal, and by the 16th century a third of the wine shipped into Bristol was Spanish. This including a fortified nutty flavoured type from the province of Jerez de la Frontera, now known the world over as sherry, the Anglicised form of Jerez. Trade with the Iberian Peninsular expanded further during the 17th century, and in 1643 we find the first mention of the name 'Bristol Milk', being used to describe sherry, recognising the fact that the port was by then its major distribution centre. Indeed, one commentator went as far as saying that 'some will have called it Milk, because such wine is the first moisture given infants in this city', while in 1668, during a visit to Bristol, Samuel Pepys recounted how he was given 'plenty of good wine, and above all Bristol Milk'.

This, together with other wines and spirits, was stored in the labyrinth of ancient cellars that extended out beneath Bristol's streets, and according to Pepys much of the goods trans-

ported around the city were carried in carts drawn by dogs to prevent vibration from reaching the subterranean vaults. In spite of the Civil War, Bristol's wine trade continued to prosper, ensuring that local merchants such as J.R. Phillips & Company, founded back in 1789; Avery's

(1793); John Harvey & Sons Ltd. (1796); Wyld & Company (1803); Bartlett & Hobbs Ltd. (1825); Spackman & Gosling (1834); Dunlop, Mackie & Company (1846) and Moran's, all long established firms, were still actively trading during the 20th century.

John Harvey & Sons Ltd.

Of all Bristol's wine merchants and bottlers, Harveys is probably the most famous worldwide, and, although 'Bristol Milk' is a generic term, 'Bristol Cream' is exclusive to the company, having been one of the first trademarks to be registered back in 1882.

The firm's origins can in fact be traced back to around 1796 when William Perry & Company began trading as wine and brandy merchants from premises in Orchard Street and nearby Denmark Street. In about 1806 Thomas Urch, son of a nearby baker, was taken on as an apprentice, and in 1822 his nephew, the 16-year-old John Harvey, also joined the company. In spite of having descended from an established Cornish seafaring family, Harvey's bouts of severe seasickness

The premises of John Harvey & Sons Ltd at 12 Denmark Street, taken during the 1960s.

In the Denmark Street cellars of John Harvey & Sons Ltd.

and the drowning of his grandparents had convinced him that his best option was to stay firmly on dry land!

Although William Perry was dead by the time Harvey arrived, the company retained its original name until 1825, when Urch was joined by Edward Pritchard, son of a Kidderminster wine merchant. In 1834 John Harvey was also accepted into the partnership, after which the firm's title changed to Urch, Prichard and Harvey. Thomas Urch was then able to retire, allowing Sir William White, a wine merchant in Clifton, to join the company, and although his name added prestige to the undertaking, in 1842 John Harvey became the senior partner, as the new name of Harvey & White reflected.

John Harvey was a cultivated man who lived with his wife and eight children in Denmark Street, over the shop, until, in the 1850s, he moved to a house in Redland Park. Two of his sons, John and Edward, were not only given a strict education in preparation for joining the firm, but were also sent to learn the finer points of the wine business by meeting the growers and shippers in

Bordeaux and Jerez, as well as in Epernay, the home of champagne. Consequently, by the time their father died in 1879 they were competent enough to take over the firm, which since 1871 had been known as John Harvey & Sons.

In 1860 wine duties in Britain had been reformed, and, as a new and increasingly affluent middle class emerged, John Harvey II became increasingly successful in obtaining orders from such places as army and navy messes, gentleman's clubs and the universities, in addition to filling the cellars upwardly mobile private individuals. In 1884 the firm began exporting, and their solid success led to the formation of a limited liability company in 1893 with John Harvey II as chairman, while two years later they were granted a prestigious Royal Warrant. As well as heading the company, John Harvey II was a prominent churchman who actively promoted the building

Bottling at Harveys' Denmark Street headquarters during the 1930s.

of St Mary's church close to his own home in Leigh Woods. He also involved himself in civic affairs, serving Bristol not only as an Alderman but also as Sheriff, and as a member of the Docks Committee.

John Harvey II died in 1900, leaving his brother Edward to take over the position of chairman. Although during the early part of the 20th century prices remained static, the volume of trade rose steadily, and as claret had dropped out of fashion and sherry was considered bad for the liver vintage port became the biggest seller. The company's customer base was also changing, and as more and more people discovered the delights of wine drinking, supplying wines in bulk to large landowners and wealthy gentlemen gave way to way to selling individual bottles to the general public. Consequently, in 1908 Harveys began advertising their products, while at the same time the export trade to America became increasingly more important.

Edward remained as chairman until 1910, when his place was taken by John Harvey III, always known as 'Mr Russell', who revolutionised the company's finances and brought in new investment. He also steered the company through World War One when long hours of overtime had to be worked in order to maintain supplies to the naval and military messes, and, in particular, to military hospitals, where red burgundy or claret was often prescribed. The war, however, took its toll and an ailing and exhausted John Harvey III died in 1919, his brother Edward, who was universally known as Eddy, then being appointed chairman, a position he held until 1938.

The introduction of Prohibition in America in 1919 was something that slowed, rather than halted, Harveys' rate of expansion, and after it was finally repealed in 1933, for the first time in the 20th century, the sales of sherry overtook those of port. In spite of the Depression, the company continued to flourish and during the 1930s introduced modern labelling, capsule fitting and filling machines, which enabled them to speed up the flow of wine into the bottles without impairing its quality. In 1938 Eddy Harvey at last retired and handed the chair to his nephew, John IV, better known to everyone as 'Mr Jack', who arrived just in time to deal with the difficulties of war, the first of which involved the

HARVEYS
of Bristol
Established in 1796 Blenders & Shippers of Sherries Importers of Fine Table Wines
John Harvey & Sons Ltd. Denmark Street, Bristol

destruction of the Denmark Street premises by German bombs during the course of the first large scale raid on Bristol in November 1940. This forced Harveys to move to temporary premises in nearby Pipe Lane, and it was to be 1954 before they were able to return to their original site. In the meantime, Mr Jack had spent a great deal of time overseas, particularly in the United States, drumming up business for the company, before retiring due to ill health in 1956 and handing over the chairmanship to Edward Harvey's grandson, George McWatters.

Only 34 years of age when he took control of Harveys, McWatters time in charge was characterised by meteoric expansion. This began in 1958 when, in order to finance the construction of a new home for the company, shares were offered on the open market. Having raised a considerable amount of money, in October 1960 a massive bottling plant was opened at Whitchurch, on the outskirts of Bristol, where as many as 3,550 dozen bottles an hour could be filled. George McWatters also presided over the purchase of the old established family port firm of Cockburn Smithes in 1962, this Oporto based undertaking having been supplying Harveys since the early 19th century.

The Cockburns acquisition was a great success, but the company's excellent performance eventually began attracting hostile attention, and this culminated in January 1966 when Harveys was taken over by the Shepton Mallet-based cider and wine group, Showerings Vine Products & Whiteways. As part of the Showerings group, for the first time in its history the firm was headed by a chairman from outside the Harvey family, the

In the early days of John Harvey & Sons, a French lady was being shown around the cellars in Bristol when she came upon John Harvey, the senior partner, who asked her opinion of two sherries. The first was their famous Bristol Milk and the second, an even finer older wine. She was a good enough judge to appreciate quality. 'If that is Bristol Milk' she said, 'then this must be the Cream. It really is creme de la creme.' And so, Bristol Cream, the first cream sherry, was named.

HARVEYS BRISTOL CREAM

12 Denmark Street, Bristol.
Tel: Bristol 27665.

Bottling in Harveys' new plant at Whitchurch. This photograph was taken during the late 1960s.

sold across the globe was theirs, and making 'Bristol Cream' the world's best-selling brand. Sadly, in 1990 bottling was moved to Spain and Portugal and the Whitchurch plant closed, while in 1996 Harveys became part of the spirits and wines sector of Allied Domecq plc., whose headquarters was at Bedminster Down in Bristol. Although the company's marketing was moved to Horsham in West Sussex, the family's distinguished name continued to be seen in Bristol until early 2003, when Harveys famous restaurant and wine cellars in Denmark Street closed their doors for the last time.

Brewing

Although J.R. Phillips & Company, a firm founded in 1789 and one which operated from premises in 18/19 Nelson Street from 1810 until 1960, established a fine reputation for the quality of their 'Old Bristol Dry Gin', the same could certainly not be said of many of the concoctions on sale during the late 18th and early 19th centuries. While Sir Ernest Hook, who analysed Phillips 'Old Bristol Dry Gin' in 1935, declared it to be 'free from sugar extractives and mineral matter, and possesses valuable medicinal properties', by the

new man appointed being Francis Showering, whose nephew Keith became the Managing Director. Change was now the order of the day, and in 1968 Showerings merged with the Allied Breweries Group, giving Harveys 'captive' access to many thousands of pubs and off-licences, thus strengthening their hold on the domestic market and allowing other important acquisitions to be made.

This made Harveys the largest sherry company in the world, ensuring that one bottle in every five

Georges Bristol Brewery looking across the River Avon, *c*.1938.

1820s the damaging social effects of the widespread consumption of cheap rot-gut gin had encouraged the governments of the day to elevate the importance of beer drinking in controlled premises.

Fortunately, by that time the malting of barley had become reasonably efficient, and the rapidly developing coal industry was able to provide the larger brewers with sufficient amounts of fuel to fire their coppers and heat their water. Commercial brewers then began to make their presence felt by supplying more than just their own houses, while the Industrial Revolution brought mechanisation to the industry that required a capital outlay well beyond the pockets of small alehouse brewers.

Due to the generally poor quality of drinking water, beer of various strengths had for centuries already been the everyday drink for many men, women and children, and in Bristol in 1700 it was recorded that strong beer was available for just 6d a gallon, and that Bristolians drank it for breakfast, lunch and dinner. The happy tipplers did not have far to go to obtain supplies of their favourite beverage as the city boasted a more than adequate number of alehouses, for which 220 licences were granted in 1703, rising to 625 by 1754.

Georges Bristol Brewery

Of the dozens of small breweries that flourished at this period, one went on to become the largest such undertaking in the West Country, although the early years of world-famous Georges Bristol Brewery are still surrounded in a certain amount of mystery. Nevertheless, there is evidence that a brewery of some sort was operating on the original Tucker Street part of the site as early as 1567. It later passed into the hands of John Yeamans, a local brewer who, in 1636, passed the premises on to the Saunders family, large property owners, in whose hands it remained for three generations. Finally, in 1696, they sold out to John Hawkins, another local brewer, who went on to serve as mayor of Bristol in 1702, around which time he

The old Bristol Porter Brewery, *c*.1788.

An aerial view of Georges Bristol Brewery during the 1930s.

was also knighted. In 1730 it was sold to a consortium of Bristol merchants headed by Isaac Hobhouse, a wealthy slave trader, who in turn left his interest in the business to his two nephews, John and Henry Hobhouse. It was they who subsequently built the Old Porter Brewery, which was to become the basis of the modern complex.

Porter, a heavily hopped dark beer almost black in colour, was, according to legend, invented in 1722 by a Shoreditch brewer keen to imitate a popular drink mixed in the alehouses from three separate beers, a time consuming process for a busy landlord. A voracious demand was soon created for the new beer, and it became so popular with the London street market porters that the name porter was universally adopted. Although it had prodigious keeping qualities and could be brewed all the year round, porter had to be matured for several months, which meant that a great deal of capital became tied up in its manufacture. Consequently, the production of porter was restricted to the larger concerns with sufficient money and the necessary brewing capacity,

thereby giving birth to a modern commercial brewing industry.

Locally, the Porter Brewery in Bath Street prospered and passed through several hands before, in 1788, it was sold to a partnership of six local merchants headed by Philip George. The firm, which subsequently traded as the Philip George Bristol Porter & Beer Company, also acquired the free-

The famous 'Georges' Greys', French Percheon shire horses, which not only delivered the company's beer to generations of drinkers but were also Georges' registered trade mark.

hold of a malt house in Tucker Street. Philip was the elder of the two sons of William George, who had been trading as a distiller and wine merchant at 59 Baldwin Street since 1739. He and his brother James carried on in the family business until 1787 when Philip left to become a brewer and maltster, while by 1792 James was established as a hop and brandy merchant in King Street, a business in which James Phillips became a partner in 1808. Subsequently known as J.R. Phillips & Company, it went on to become the oldest surviving wine merchants in Bristol, eventually becoming a wholesale agency owned by Allied Lyons and Whitbreads operating from a site in Avonmouth.

Back at the brewery, not only did Philip George prove to be a good businessman who gave 28 years' service to the firm, but he also owned the Patent Shot Company and took a great interest in civic affairs, serving as Sheriff of Bristol in 1808, 1813 and 1815, before his death at the age of 78 in 1828. Some of his partners also had diverse com-

mercial and personal interests, but, in spite of the fact that Peter Lunnell was a prominent anti-slavery campaigner and Samuel Span held opposing views, this in no way inhibited their business collaboration!

Unfortunately, poor harvests and the outbreak of the French Revolutionary War conspired together to make the brewery unprofitable, and

Filling aluminium casks in Georges Bristol Brewery.

until 1797 it had to be kept afloat by profits from Philip George's other business ventures. Nevertheless, in 1794 the company was telling potential customers that they 'will deliver in barrels and half barrels their Porter to all towns and villages within five miles of the city and is sold at Four pence per Quart.' However, in spite of early sales of porter to Liverpool and Ireland, competition soon forced the brewery to consider diversifying, and in 1796 they opened a new pale ale brewery, which was also built in Bath Street, right alongside their original premises. An export trade was also developed, and by the mid-19th century Georges had supplied their beer to such diverse countries as the United States, Canada, Jamaica, Argentina, Portugal and India.

By this time the brewery employed about 40 people, who were working a 70-hour week, of which the coopers were the highest paid, receiving 19s 6d for a week's work. By contrast, others found themselves loosing money for bad behaviour, a one shilling fine being imposed for the use of improper language or being late on brewing morning, rising to 2s 6d for getting drunk, while one man forfeited his whole Sunday wage 'for leaving the large plug out'.

By the end of the Napoleonic War only two of the original partners remained, and in 1816 both Philip George and Jacob Wilcox Ricketts, proprietor of the Phoenix Glass House, took the decision to retire in favour of their sons, a new partnership styled Georges, Ricketts & Company being formed as a result. Richard Vaughan joined the brewery in 1827, and, following the death of

The bottling line at Georges Bristol Brewery, *c*.1938.

the last of the Ricketts family, in 1861 the firm was retitled Georges & Company, with Alfred George as senior partner. Over the years the George family remained closely connected with the brewery, and after Georges & Company became a public company in 1888 Charles George was appointed managing director, while its first chairman, Philip Vaughan, was replaced in 1890 by Charles George. Thereafter, the chairmanship of the Bristol Brewery Georges Ltd was always held by a member of the George family.

During the early part of the 19th century the drinking of gin had reached epidemic proportions, and in an effort to curb the habit the Duke of Wellington, who was then Prime Minister, introduced the Beer Act. This not only removed the duty on beer but also gave anyone the right to sell beer from their home or business premises upon the payment of an annual fee of two guineas to the Excise. This not only changed drinkers' lives but also brewers' fortunes. For the rest of the century the larger commercial breweries gradually rendered many of the traditional home and publican brewers redundant.

However, the administration of Beer Houses by the Excise was transferred back to local magistrates in 1869, after which breweries began buying up as many retail outlets as they could in order to provide them with a captive market for their own products and to limit the influence of others. Consequently, by 1888 Georges had acquired some 70 retail outlets, by which time less than 20 local brewers were supplying 88 percent of Bristol's beer. This trend towards rationalisation in the brewing industry gathered pace towards the end of the 19th century when all over the country new companies were floated, many of which were based on the amalgamation of a number of previously independent breweries. This was the case in Bristol, where in 1889 Bristol United was formed by four local firms joining together as a defence against Georges.

During the early years of the 20th century Georges was employing around 170 people, a relatively small number for such a concern. Of these, the brewing department employed 64, deliveries 30 and bottling 17. The chief brewer received £270 per annum, just £10 more than the highest paid of the travellers responsible for the tied trade! Georges was a non-union company and the directors did their beast to foster a spirit of co-operation with the workers, resulting in the introduction of a Christmas bonus for the employees in 1891. Various welfare benefits were also provided, although pensions were for many years only granted at the discretion of the board of directors, while in 1931 Georges purchased a six-acre field in West Town Lane, Brislington, which became the company's sports ground.

Two giant mash tuns in Georges Bristol Brewery, *c*.1938.

The quickest way for any brewery to increase its profits and to obtain more outlets was to buy up its smaller competitors, close down their brewing operations, sell off the site and take over their pubs. This was a policy upon which Georges embarked in 1889, when they absorbed the Bedminster Bridge Brewery, and by 1892 some 350 tied houses were in their ownership. The trend continued into the 20th century, R.W. Miller & Company of Stokes Croft being acquired in 1911; Lodway, at Pill, in 1912; J. Arnold & Sons of Wickwar and Welton Breweries in 1918; the Bath Brewery in 1923 and the Ashton Gate Brewery in 1931. These, and the individual purchase of previously 'free houses', brought the total number of pubs and off licences owned by Georges to 922 by 1936 making it one of the country's largest regional brewers. The purchase in 1932 of a controlling interest in Messrs Wyld & Company Ltd, the long established wine shippers in Redcliff Street, also proved to be a good investment.

Having taken over a number of its smaller rivals, Georges found it necessary to increase its brewing capacity to meet the demand, and an expansion of the brewery site was undertaken.

This began in 1919 when they bought the extensive Talbot Hotel premises on the corner of Bath Street and Victoria Street, and culminated in 1924 with the acquisition of a large piece of land to the east of the existing brewery, lying between the Counterslip and the River Avon. Extensive development work was then undertaken so that by the time it was completed in 1933 Georges brewery covered a three-acre site stretching almost from Bristol Bridge to St Philip's Bridge.

After World War Two Georges was left with only one real rival, Bristol United Breweries, whose leading brand nationally was the famous Oakhill Invalid Stout. Even they could not resist the pressure for rationalisation that was now picking up pace within the brewing industry, and, consequently, in 1956 they were absorbed by their larger competitor and their brewing operation in Lewin's Mead closed down. This merger not only made Georges by far the largest brewer in the south-west, but, ironically, a prime target for takeover by even larger concerns from outside the region.

Overtures were soon being made, and Georges' years of independence finally came to an end in 1961 when they were absorbed by Courage,

Courage came to Bristol

in 1961 when The Bristol Brewery Georges & Company Limited, which was founded in 1788 as *Philip George and the Bristol Porter Brewery*, joined forces with Courage Barclay & Simonds Limited of London. Now, in 1968, the famous old Bristol Brewery in Bath Street emerges from extensive redevelopment and modernisation, the largest, the most impressive brewery unit in the West of England. It needs to be big, because Bristol-brewed beer is in greater demand than ever. No wonder they say that—

COURAGE  is the word for beer

Part of Courage's old Bristol Brewery site in 2005, during the course of conversion into an up-market riverside development.

Barclay & Simonds Ltd, a company whose power base lay in south-east England, and in 1964 the Bristol Brewery Georges Ltd was re-titled Courage (Western) Ltd. Courages built a new bottling department at Avonmouth before they, in turn, were acquired in 1972 by the Imperial Tobacco Group, as part of their diversification into the food and drinks industry, and later by the Hanson Trust when they took control of Imperial.

In 1986 Hansons sold their Courage subsidiary to the Elders IXL Group, an Australian conglomerate, and as real ale was by then making a come back, Elders embarked on an extensive modernisation project, which made the Bristol operation the largest dedicated real ale brewery in the world, their main output being Director's Bitter, Courage Best and BA. In 1987 the Elders Brewery Group, as it was then known, changed its name to the Fosters Brewery Group, which in 1995 sold Courage Ltd on to Newcastle & Scottish plc.

They had very different ideas for the Bristol brewery and, in spite of promises to the contrary, closed down the whole operation in October 1999. A £17 million scheme to redevelop the old brewery site was then put in hand, and although the brew house and tower buildings were converted into 35 up-market flats, the bottling store and malt house were demolished to make way for modern brick and glass offices in what is now known as Georges Square. This left only the premises at St Brendan's Way, Avonmouth, still connected with the brewing industry, but all they housed were the headquarters of Courage (West & Wales) and Courage (Western) Ltd's distribution depot.

CHAPTER 7
Tobacco and Chocolate

STANSFIELD & COS Super-Fine Tobacco, Castle-Street BRISTOL.

Tobacco

When European explorers first arrived in North America they found the indigenous people smoking tobacco in a way that is still familiar today. They soon discovered that the native Americans believed that it had special medicinal properties, and so were keen to send samples back to Europe. It first arrived in France in 1556, and, after being introduced to Portugal and Spain, finally made its appearance in England in 1565. European settlers in the West Indies and North America then began to cultivate tobacco as a crop, this first being recorded in Cuba around 1580 and in Virginia about 1612. It proved a great success and soon became the chief commodity exchanged by the colonists for European manufactured goods.

Although a law passed in 1624 decreed that London was to have the monopoly on the importation of tobacco into England, by about 1670 half

of Bristol's ships were engaged in this trade, its geographical position making it an ideal port of entry for exports from the New World. With so much tobacco arriving in the city, by the 1750s a small industry had grown up involving a number of individual tobacconists concentrated around the Castle Street, Peter Street and Old Market Street area. From these humble beginnings sprang a firm that was to make Bristol the largest tobacco importing and manufacturing centre in the country, a position it still held at the outbreak of World War Two.

W.D. & H.O. Wills

It all began at 73 Castle Street where, in 1786, Samuel Watkins, one of 14 tobacconists in the city, took into partnership one Henry Overton Wills, a 25-year-old member of a Salisbury clockmaking family. The firm was initially known as Wills, Watkins & Company, but in 1789 Watkins retired, leaving H.O. Wills to carry on alone for a few years, during which time he traded as Wills &

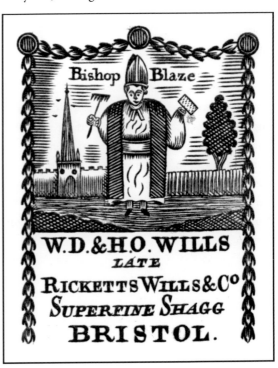

Bishop Blaze
W.D.&H.O. WILLS LATE RICKETTS WILLS&CO SUPERFINE SHAGG BRISTOL.

W.D. & H.O. Wills's premises at 112 Redcliff Street. It was first used by the firm in 1791.

Company. By that time his kindly attitude towards his eight workers was already being demonstrated by inviting them, four at a time, to dine with him on alternative Sundays. Thus began a tradition that Wills were among the most enlightened employers in the country, and that working for the company usually meant a job for life.

In 1791 H.O. Wills went into partnership with Peter Lilly to form Lilly & Wills, the business being conducted from Lilly's existing premises at 112 Redcliff Street. This continued until 1803 when Lilly retired and Samuel Ditchett took his place, the new undertaking trading as Wills & Ditchett. In 1805 they purchased the snuff mill at Stapleton, which the company had been leasing since 1792, and exactly 10 years later H.O. Wills's two sons, William Day Wills and Henry Overton Wills junior, were brought into the firm, which was then known as Wills, Ditchett & Company. The company's founder, H.O. Wills, died in 1826, and upon the retirement of Samuel Ditchett in 1830 the two Wills brothers took control of the family firm. In 1833 they were joined by Frederick Ricketts, who conducted a similar business in Mary-le-Port Street, where Ricketts, Wills & Company subsequently concentrated their snuff-making activities.

Frederick Ricketts finally retired in 1843, after which the firm was re-titled W.D. & H.O. Wills, reflecting the fact that for the first time in many years the family were the sole proprietors. They immediately started to expand and develop the business, and during the 1840s began advertising their 'Wills Best', 'Birds Eye' and 'Bishop's Blaze Shag', all of which were pipe tobaccos. The steady growth continued, and by 1855 W.D. & H.O. Wills were manufacturing 'Superfine', 'Dutch Cut' 'Turkey', 'Orinoco', Virginia Returns', 'Real Varmas', 'Real Latakia', 'Real Yara', 'Cut Cavendish', 'Bright Red Rag', 'Fine Birds Eye', 'Shag Birds Eye', 'Bogie Roll', 'Alloa Roll', 'Negrohead' and 'Real Havanah', making them a household name all over the world.

The two Wills brothers were members of the Penn Street Tabernacle, and as ardent nonconformists they insisted that their employees also be active members of a Sunday School. However, this should not imply that they were stern killjoys, for in 1851 they dispatched a party of 120 employees by horse bus and train to the Great Exhibition in London, each having been given a sovereign as spending money! The firm was also extremely loyal to their employees, and although the American Civil War was to cause a downturn in business, H.O. Wills junior dismissed any talk of making workers redundant by saying 'I can't do that. These men have wives and children to support. I'll pawn my shirt first.'

Notwithstanding troubles in America, demand for the company's products had increased to such an extent that in 1865 Wills set up a factory in London, while during 1869 and 1870 the Redcliff Street site was completely rebuilt. During this work, great care was taken to ensure they offered a good working environment, and a little over 10 years later a report was still praising their layout. 'Looking at these trim and tidy girls with smiling faces and nimble fingers, one somehow instinc-

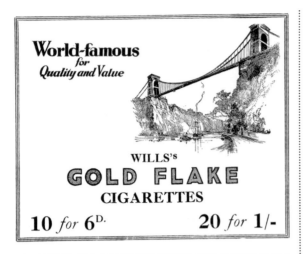

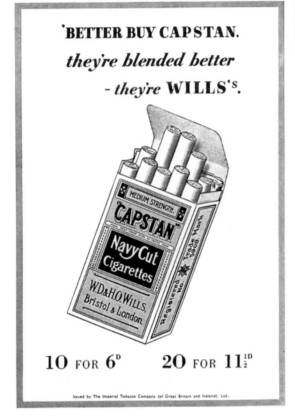

Bristol Byzantine-style office block remained in use until the early 1960s.

W.D. Wills died in 1865 and his younger brother, H.O. Wills junior, in 1871, by which time the company was headed by William Henry Wills, who had joined the family firm back in 1847. Times were now changing in the tobacco trade as cigarettes, which had first been discovered by troops during the Crimean War, were just starting to become popular, something Wills were quick to appreciate. Consequently, in 1871 they began marketing their first brand, 'Bristol', which was originally made at the London factory. It proved to be a winner and remained in production until 1974.

In the years that followed cigarettes became an increasingly more important part of Wills' business, and their popularity was largely responsible for the firm's spectacular growth during the last quarter of the 19th century. Other brands quickly followed, including such classics as 'Passing Cloud' in 1874 and 'Three Castles' in 1878, while in 1883 Harry Wills, grandson of the founder, acquired the British patent for the American Bonsak machine. This could produce 1,500 cigarettes in eight minutes, a number that would have taken an operative all day to produce by hand. The new machines slashed production costs dramatically and lead to the introduction in 1888 of 'Wild Woodbines' at a price of five for 1d, ensuring that the brand became one of Wills' most famous.

By 1880 the company were employing some 600 people in Bristol and London, and in order to keep up with demand Wills Virginia Cavendish Works was opened in Baldwin Street in 1883. Further expansion quickly followed and, as the extended Redcliff Street factory was still proving too small, in March 1886 production began in what became known as the No.1 Factory in East Street, Bedminster. It was designed by Frank Wills who ensured that each department was provided with its own dining room and kitchen. Although it was initially described as 'the finest and most complete tobacco factory in the United Kingdom', by 1908 it had been found necessary to extend the

tively feels that the system adopted must have a wonderful influence, for these are as far removed from the Midland and Northern factory hands as can be imagined. The arrangements for the comfort and convenience of the workpeople shows the thoughtful concern that Messrs. Wills have for them. On the various landings there are lavatories and a dressing room, for both men and women, and a library to which all have access.' The premises went on to serve the company well, and although the factory portion closed in 1929 the premises further down the street. In the meantime what was to be No.4 Factory was opened at Ashton Gate, followed in 1906 by No.3 Factory in nearby Raleigh Road.

The 2,000 Wills employees enjoyed excellent working conditions, although the process of selection was strict, requiring female applicants to provide suitable Sunday school references, to pass a sewing test for dexterity and to sign indentures, which promised that they would 'not contract matrimony within the said term, or play at cards or dice.' The company also offered a number of much sought after apprenticeships to boys, and at the end of the 19th century they earned 2 shillings a week for the first year, which rose to 6 shillings during their fifth year.

In addition to offering an almost unmatched working environment, the employees were also treated to annual summer outings, and in 1891 the factory girls' wages were increased, the working hours reduced to 8am to 6pm and one week's paid holiday provided for those with a year's service. By 1893 Wills had become the model employer, having established its own fire brigade, a brass band, a library, a savings bank, a recreation hall and theatre, a gym, a sports ground, a medical and dental service, a convalescent home down by the sea at Clevedon and introduced subsidised meals for its workforce.

In 1901 Wills allied itself with 12 other family-run tobacco manufacturers in Britain to form Imperial Tobacco Ltd in order to combat the giant American Tobacco Company, which wanted to extend its influence to Britain. The first chairman of the new consortium was none other than Sir William Henry Wills Bt., who later became Lord Winterstoke and headed the largest and most profitable of the merging firms. With W.D. & H.O. Wills and Nottingham-based John Player &

Two of the three large tobacco bonds still surviving close to the Cumberland Basin. Owned by the Port of Bristol Authority and built betwen 1905 and 1908, these were used to store tobacco until required by the manufacturers. Only then would the necessary duty be paid to HM Customs & Excise.

Sons as the group's main shareholders, manufacturing also took place in Swindon, Belfast, Glasgow and Newcastle, while Imperial's acquisition of Ogdens the following year added Liverpool to the list of sites.

By the time of the outbreak of World War One the Imperial Tobacco Group was well established and had just launched the famous 'Embassy' brand, and although cigarette consumption fell initially as a result of the post war depression it increased steadily again from 1924. Throughout much of the 20th century Wills continued to provide some of the most secure jobs in Bristol, with pay and conditions superior to that offered by the majority of the city's employers. During the 1930s men were still expected to wear a collar and tie and look neat and clean, and while unmarried women of any age had to call the foreman 'Mister' as a special concession married ladies were permitted to address him by his Christian name. Employees who demonstrated good time keeping throughout the year were rewarded with a Christmas bonus, and anyone who worked a machine for three years without a break received an additional payment of 10s 6d a week. In return the employees were expected to work hard, with the 600 girls engaged in stripping tobacco by hand at the Ashton Gate factory being required to strip at least 80 lbs a day, while those making cigarettes were often exposed

The East Street, Bedminster, headquarters of W.D. & H.O. Wills during Edwardian times.

Men working inside one of Bristol's tobacco bonds.

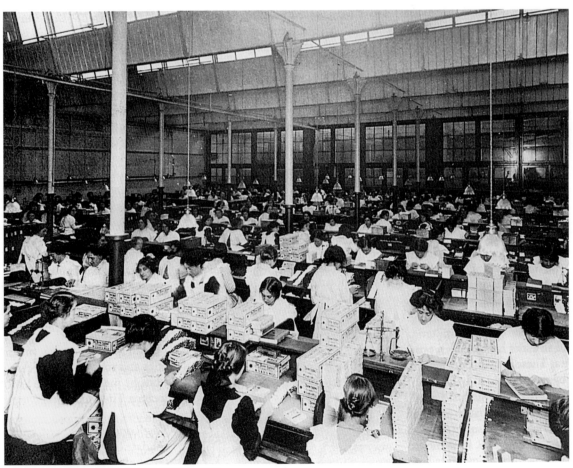

Cigarette packing at W.D. & H.O. Wills in 1919.

WILL'S's
Wild Woodbine
Cigarettes

W. D. & H. O. WILLS.

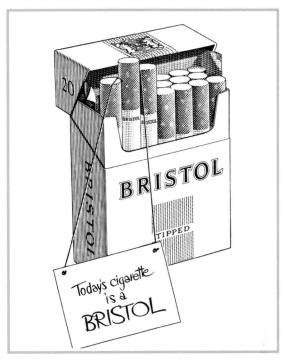

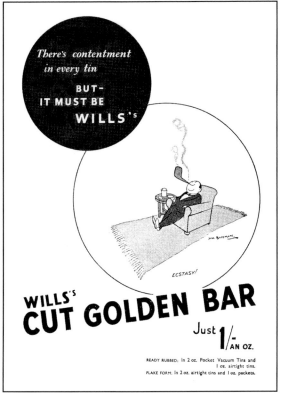

to clouds of choking tobacco dust as they blew out their machines using hand bellows.

As smoking habits changed Imperial adapted, with 'Castella Panatella' cigars being introduced in 1937 and tipped versions of 'Woodbines', 'Capstan Medium' and 'Gold Flake' appearing for the first time in 1949. The group then began to consider diversifying into food, drink and leisure, and this eventually began during the 1960s through the acquisition of such established concerns as the HP Sauce Group, Golden Wonder, Smedley's and the brewers Courage Ltd. To reflect this change of direction the company was renamed the Imperial Group Ltd, while a totally owned subsidiary known as Imperial Tobacco Ltd was formed to handle just the tobacco products.

The East Street, Bedminster, headquarters of W.D. & H.O. Wills, photographed in about 1920.

By the late 1960s it was obvious that the old Wills factories in Bristol were seriously outdated, so in order to be able to introduce the latest production methods it was decided to transfer manufacturing to a totally new facility. Consequently, in 1969 the Redcliff Street premises were demolished, and two years later work began on a £15 million factory at Hartcliffe, which was subsequently constructed on a 57-acre site. The first cigarettes were produced there in 1973, and

within two years the majority of the Wills operation had been transferred out of the Bedminster and Ashton areas.

At its peak in the late 1970s Hartcliffe was the largest tobacco factory in Europe, employing 4,500 people and producing some 350 million cigarettes a week. The production hall was a remarkable piece of civil engineering as it had no internal supports, which made it one of the finest unobstructed spaces in any British factory. In

keeping with Wills benevolent traditions, the staff were provided with their own supermarket, post office, bus station, medical centre, dentist, bank and six restaurants.

The Imperial Group, which abolished the Wills board in 1981, survived until April 1986 when it was taken over by the Hanson Trust, an organisation that quickly separated the food, drink and leisure elements of the business from tobacco. This left Imperial Tobacco Ltd, which had its headquarters at Hartcliffe, to concentrate on its traditional business. Not surprisingly, rationalisation soon took place, and although in October 1991 the Hartcliffe factory was closed and cigarette production moved to Nottingham, cigar making was transferred from Glasgow to a new factory at Winterstoke Road. Likewise, the headquarters of Imperial Tobacco Ltd moved to the Southville area of Bristol and their Southern Trading Division down to Avonmouth.

Between the time of its foundation and the late 1960s some 30 members of the Wills family were connected with the business, and three of these went on to serve as Sheriffs of Bristol. Fortunately, over the years the company generated huge profits for them, and although some was used for the

the best in smoking
WILLS ⚜
pacemakers in tobacco

An aerial view of Imperial Tobacco's Hartcliffe factory.

Manufacturing cigarettes in Imperial Tobacco's Hartcliffe Factory.

benefit of the employees considerable sums were spent for the benefit of Bristolians in general. In common with several other local industrialists, Bristol's fledgling university was a cause close to the heart of the Wills family, and their generosity ensured not only its successful foundation but also its subsequent development. In so doing they gave Bristol one of its finest landmarks, the Wills

During 1986–87 most of W.D. & H.O. Wills premises in East Street, Bedminster, were demolished, leaving only the façade of the 1884 No.1 Factory flanked by two later sections. These now form the frontage of an arcade, behind which is to be found a row of small retail businesses.

Tower at the top of Park Street, which houses 'Great George', the fourth largest bell in England.

The nearby Museum and Art Gallery also benefited from the dynasty's generosity, as did the Homeopathic Hospital, St Monica's home for the elderly, the Theatre Royal, the Cabot Tower and at least 30 churches, including St Mary Redcliff, for which money was provided to enable important restoration work to be undertaken. These will perhaps be the most lasting monuments to an industry that was once so important to Bristol, as the shell of the old East Street factory, which was gutted back in 1986, now houses only shops, while one of the Ashton factories has become an arts centre. Even less remains at Hartcliffe where the massive factory was demolished in 1999 to make way for a £30 million shopping complex and industrial park.

Chocolate

Chocolate arrived in England in 1657 when a Frenchman opened a shop in London where solid chocolate, the basic ingredient for the drink, could be purchased at between 10 and 15 shillings per pound. Its extremely high price ensured that only the wealthy could afford such a luxury, but nevertheless fashionable chocolate houses where the hot beverage could be sipped soon began to appear in the major European cities, spurred on by the belief that drinking chocolate also possessed important medicinal properties.

That beverage, however, still retained all its

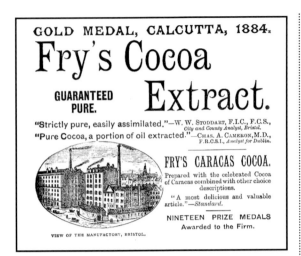

natural fat or cocoa butter, and it was not until the introduction of hydraulic presses in 1828 that the dry cocoa powder as we know it today made its first appearance. However, the high import duty upon raw cocoa beans continued to be levied in Britain, and this prevented chocolate products from becoming universally popular until it was finally reduced to a uniform rate of 1d per pound in 1853. The introduction of cocoa trees from South America to West Africa in 1873 also increased the availability of beans in this country and further helped to boost the local industry.

J.S. Fry & Company

For many years the largest and most famous of Britain's chocolate manufacturers was located in central Bristol, and that company, J.S. Fry & Sons Ltd, could also trace its foundation back to the first quarter of the 18th century, making it the oldest in the country. The original business was established in 1728 in Narrow Wine Street by a Bristol apothecary, Walter Churchman, who, three years later, took out a patent 'for the sole use of an Engine for expeditious, fine and clean making of chocolate in greater perfection'. This water-powered machine enabled him to produce chocolate much more finely ground than most producers could manage by hand, ensuring that his firm was able to maintain an independent existence until the death of Churchman's son, Charles, after which the business was taken over by Dr Joseph Fry in 1761.

Fry had been born into a devout Quaker fam-

J. S. FRY & SONS LTD.,

Manufacturers by Special Warrants of Appointment to

H.M. KING EDWARD VII.   H.I.M. THE EMPRESS EUGENIE.
H.M. QUEEN ALEXANDRA.   H.M. THE KING OF SPAIN.
H.R.H. THE PRINCE OF WALES.   H.M. THE QUEEN OF SPAIN.

Also to

H.M. The late QUEEN VICTORIA.   H.I.M. The late EMPEROR NAPOLEON

WHEN you see a new food advertised, you try it out of curiosity. You're experimenting. When you buy Fry's Pure Concentrated Cocoa, you are upholding the judgment of several generations of Englishmen and Englishwomen who lived through the most strenuous times of our island history. Nearly a century before Wellington won Waterloo, or Nelson gained for us the freedom of the seas,

Fry's
Cocoas and Chocolates

had been used in English homes. There's no experimenting with Fry's.

THE HISTORIC HOUSE,

ESTABLISHED IN THE REIGN OF KING GEORGE II., 1728.

ily in Sutton Benger in Wiltshire, and, after serving an apprenticeship with an apothecary in Basingstoke, he moved to Bristol where he set up in business in Small Street in 1756. As chocolate was still considered to have health-giving quali-

FRY'S MILK CHOCOLATE

DESPERATION. PACIFICATION. EXPECTATION. ACCLAMATION. REALIZATION
ITS FRY'S

J.S. FRY & SONS Lᵀᴰ, BRISTOL & LONDON.

ties, Joseph Fry began manufacturing it himself and it was not long before it became the most important part of his trade, encouraging him to expand his business by moving to Narrow Wine Street in 1759 and buying out Walter Churchman two years later.

As his business expanded Fry built up a network of agents, selling his products in some 53 towns up and down the country. The increasing demand for his chocolate continued, and in 1777 he moved to newly constructed premises in Union Street, which was to be the firm's home for the next 150 years. Here he continued to produce a crude form of chocolate, which the customer would take home, scrape into a jug and then boil up with milk or water to produce the drink.

Joseph Fry continued to run his chocolate business until his death in 1787 at the age of 59, after which it

passed to his wife Anna, trading as Anna Fry & Sons, and, upon her retirement in 1795, to their youngest son, Joseph Storrs Fry. He immediately embarked upon a policy of expansion and mechanisation, but this proved very costly, forcing him in 1805 to take Dr Henry Hunt, a fellow Quaker, as a partner. Following the injection of Hunt's capital the company again prospered, and, although the Fry & Hunt partnership was dissolved in 1822 when the latter retired, during the

A drawing of Fry's factories in Central Bristol, *c.*1880.

A drawing of girls weighing and filing packets of cocoa at Fry's Union Street factory in 1884.

By the 1840s public taste was shifting away from the very sweet drinking chocolate towards cocoa, which contained less sugar, and in 1847 Fry's pioneered the introduction of eating chocolate in Britain. This was followed in 1853 by chocolate covered 'Cream Sticks', the first chocolate confectionery ever to be made on a factory scale, and in 1866 these became the famous 'Cream Bars', which went on to become one of Fry's most famous and long-lived products. The reduction in import duty on the firm's raw materials and improved manufacturing techniques did much to dramatically reduce the cost of Fry's products, a good example being best chocolate, which fell from 7s 6d per pound in 1771 to just 11d by the mid-1850s.

New blood was now injected into the firm, Joseph Fry II's son, Joseph Storrs Fry III, being made a partner in 1854, followed by Francis's son, Francis James Fry, in 1858. With the younger generation established in the company, Joseph Fry II felt able to retire in 1867, followed by Francis in 1878, the same year in which his brother Richard passed away. This left the two cousins in sole control of J.S. Fry & Company, and in 1880 they brought into the partnership Joseph Storrs Fry II's nephew, Albert. The favourable market conditions that prevailed in Britain during the latter part of the 19th century ensured that Fry's continued to prosper, and in 1885 the sales of eating chocolate overtook those of cocoa.

Exports also rose steadily, in particular to countries within the British Empire, encouraging the company to embark on another expansion programme. This resulted in the firm opening seven new factories in central Bristol between 1860 and 1907, of which the largest was that erected in 1878 at the bottom of Pithay. The same period also saw an increase in employee numbers, these rising from some 200 in the late 1860s to about 4,500 by the turn of the century, and in January 1896 the business became a private limited company with Joseph Storrs Fry II as Chairman. At that time the company had eight factories in the area bounded by Tower Lane, Nelson Street, Broadmead, Union Street, and

following year Fry's were using nearly 40 percent of all the cocoa imported into Britain.

Fry then brought his three sons, Joseph II, Francis and Richard, into the business but retained control of what was now J.S. Fry & Sons until his death in 1835, at which time the firm was employing some 16 people. Advertising campaigns were then run, and with growing profits in 1840 the brothers were able to begin work on a new factory, building on their existing Union Street site, in which some 28 different chocolate products were soon being manufactured.

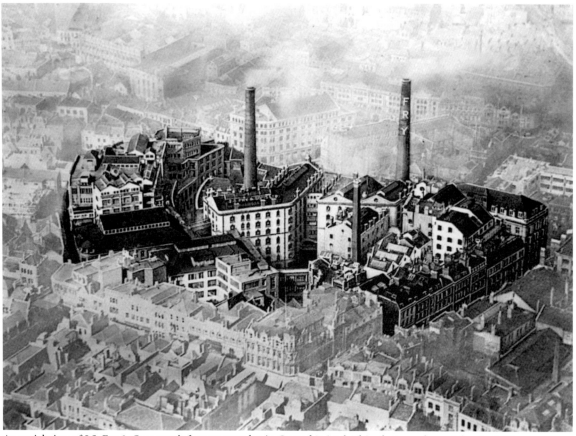

An aerial view of J.S. Fry & Company's factory complex in Central Bristol. This photograph was taken in 1924.

The main office building in J.S. Fry & Company's Union Street factory complex.

Wine Street, with off-shoots in Quay Street, St George's Street, Whapping Wharf and Cumberland Road.

From the time of its foundation it was 'in grained in the Fry's foremen not to look upon their employees as so many cogs in a machine for producing dividends, but as human creatures possessed of immortal souls, for whom they were very largely responsible'. This Quaker view of benevolent paternalism led the company to provide their employees with welfare benefits that few other firms could rival, including their own chapel and schoolroom, the provision of night-school teachers and facilities in which various clubs and societies could meet. Their premises in Union Street were visited by Government inspectors during the 1860s, who found that there was no overcrowding and that the place was 'strikingly clean and comfortable'.

About 200 people were employed there, of which over 130 were women, half of these being

'A' Block under construction at Fry's new Somerdale factory. This photograph was taken in 1922.

girls under the age of 18. In comparison, only a small number of boys worked in the factory, none of whom were under the age of 12. The female employees, who were mostly found to have been responsible for packing, filling bags, fastening and labelling the packages, worked only from 8am until 6pm, as Joseph Storrs Fry considered it 'better to let them take their breakfast comfortably at home'. However, this privilege was not extended to the men and boys, who were expected to work through from 6am until 6pm, with a half-hour break for lunch. Every day the whole workforce was expected to attend a short religious service at 8.45am, and although Saturday was also a working day the factory closed early at 2pm.

Fry's took a great interest in their individual employees, all of whom were expected to be Christian, teetotal, punctual and to arrive in clean working clothes. To encourage this, bonuses were paid to good timekeepers, while those who arrived late could expect to be fined. Singing, consuming the company's products or slipping into beer shops during working hours was strictly forbidden, and 'no persons, however skilful, are retained whose moral conduct is unsatisfactory'. The literacy rate among the workers was high as a result of Fry's enthusiasm for education, and so it

was possible for the firm to present any girl who left to get married with a copy of 'Mrs Beeton's Book of Household Management'. Wages were also good by local standards, with girls being paid between 3 and 5 shillings a week, while women could expect to receive between 7 and 10 shillings.

At the start of the 20th century chocolate manufacturers in Britain were experiencing stiff competition from Swiss producers, who had brought milk chocolate on to the market, and J.S. Fry & Sons Ltd responded by being the first company in this country to market its own version. This was introduced in 1902 and 'Five Boys Milk Chocolate', which survived until 1976, soon became one of the country's best known brands through its advertisement that showed a young boy's face passing through five expressions, from sorrow to joy, as he ate Fry's chocolate (Desperation, Pacification, Expectation, Acclamation, Realisation ....It's Fry). The young man in question was five-year-old Lindsay Poulton, who had originally been pho-

Chocolate packing at J.S. Fry & Sons.

tographed back in 1886 and the images used on show cards, enamel panels and in newspapers, before the introduction of 'Five Boys', after which his face became irretrievably connected with the famous bar.

During the 1900s the aged Joseph Storrs Fry II remained chairman, a position he held up until his death in 1913. This limited the power of others within the firm to become more aggressive in their advertising and to move out of their

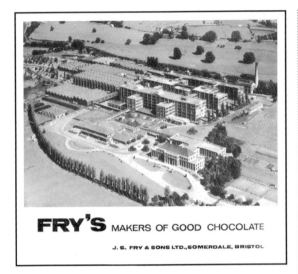

cramped and fragmented site in central Bristol, thereby making it difficult to respond effectively to increasing competition from Cadburys and Rowntrees. Nevertheless, 1914 did see the introduction of another famous product, Fry's Turkish Delight. World War One then intervened, and as the conflict progressed the three companies gradually drew closer together, united in the difficult trading conditions brought on by shortages of imported raw materials. Finally, with the arrival on the scene of Nestlé and with Fry's position becoming progressively weaker, in 1917 the management agreed to a merge with Cadburys.

Consequently, in October 1918 the two firms became subsidiaries of a holding company known as the British Cocoa & Chocolate Company, of which Barrow Cadbury became chairman and Richard A. Fry vice-chairman, reflecting that, in reality, control resided with the Cadbury board at Bourneville. At that time Fry's manufacturing facilities were completely outdated, and as they were spread between 16 different factories situated in central Bristol, all of which were hemmed in on all sides and lacked any direct rail or water communication, the decision was made to relocate.

This did not take long to arrange, and in 1923 the company moved to a completely new factory complex built on a 228-acre green field site some six miles away at Keynsham, its name Somerdale having been chosen by national competition! Masterminded by Major Egbert Cadbury and Cecil Roderick Fry, the move from Union Street took until 1935 to complete, and at its height the

A SOUVENIR OF SOMERDALE

modern blocks at Somerdale were providing employment for over 5,000 people. Demolition work on Fry's old factories in Bristol began in 1932, although it was the early 1960s before the two well-known chimneys at the Pithay site were finally brought down.

Continuing in the Quaker traditions of both the Fry and Cadbury families, the employees at Somerdale enjoyed subsidised meals, medical services and good pension schemes, as well as being provided with playing fields and facilities for such social activities as amateur dramatics, music and photography. To complete the process of integration, in 1935 Fry's finally became a wholly owned subsidiary of Cadbury Ltd, and following massive reorganisation, which began in the 1960s, the production of a range of sugar confectionery products, such as Sharps, Pascall, Murray, Trebor, Bassett, and Maynard, were transferred to Somerdale. Although the name of Fry's ceased to be used at Somerdale in 1981, the factory remained a major production unit of Cadbury Ltd, the Confectionery Division of Cadbury Schweppes Ltd, and two of the original

products, Fry's Chocolate Cream and Fry's Turkish Delight still continued to be manufactured.

H.J. Packer & Company

In spite of the excellent working conditions and good rates of pay, not everyone was content to remain working for Fry's, and by the outbreak of World War One two other locally-based chocolate makers had become established. Although the purpose built Weber Chocolate Company's factory at Lodge Causeway in Fishponds remained in production only from 1913 until 1965, H.J. Packer & Company, its older and better known competitor, proved to be an altogether more successful and long-lived enterprise.

The firm's origins can be traced back to 1881 when a Mr Packer, who had previously been employed by J.S. Fry & Sons, started a chocolate manufacturing company under his own name. He began trading at 46 Armoury Square, Easton, and was soon joined by his brother and sister and a Miss Lily Brown. To begin with wages were as low as 2s 6d per week, and heating and lighting sup-

The Lodge Causeway, Fishponds, factory of the Weber Chocolate Company as it appeared during the 1930s.

The old Weber chocolate factory awaiting new occupiers in 2005.

plied only by the kitchen fire and paraffin lamps, but soon Packers was able to take over the house next door, so beginning the company's expansion. By 1883 he had entered into partnership with Mr H.J. Burrows, another ex-employee of J.S. Fry & Sons, and the following year moved to new premises on the corner of Orange Street and St Paul Street in St Paul's.

The partnership, however, was short lived and in 1885 it was dissolved, leaving Burrows, who

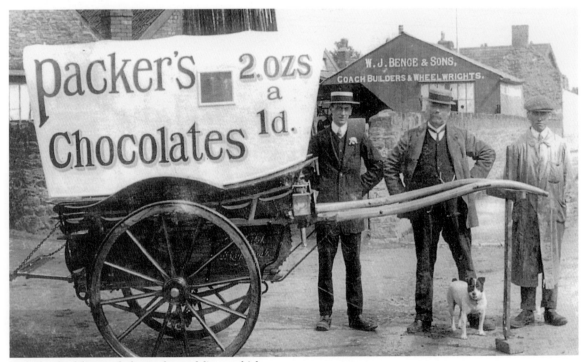

Packer's take delivery of a horse-drawn delivery vehicle.

Packer's Greenbank factory shortly after opening in 1902.

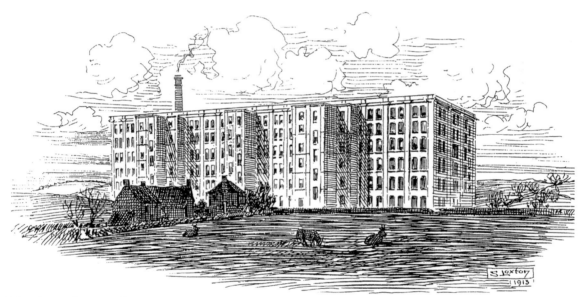

A drawing made in 1913 by S. Loxton showing Carson's new Shortwood factory.

then injected his initials into the firms title, as sole proprietor. Yet another change took place in 1886 when the firm of H.J. Packer and Company,

Chocolate and Cocoa Manufacturers was purchased for £950 by Bruce Cole, who retained the company name. By 1892 the firm had expanded enough to be able to open a sales office in London, while wages in the factory had increased to 4s 6d a week, making many of the workers consider themselves to be well paid. The normal working day at this time lasted from 8am until 6pm, but if trade was particularly brisk a 6am start was not unusual. Mechanisation was also introduced during the 1890s, the first machine to arrive being put to work coating Packers' 'Two Ounces a Penny' chocolates. So successful were these that by the end of the decade nearly 40 were in use.

Packers' Playing Field Pavillion was used as a military hospital during World War One.

With business booming the St Paul's premises were proving too cramped, and so in 1900 the company purchased land at Greenbank, where they consequently constructed a new three-block factory powered by steam engines. Production was moved there in 1902 and by 1912 Packers sales had increased by 250 percent, allowing them not only to form a subsidiary company known as Charles Bond, which was to specialise in high class chocolate products, but also to acquire a controlling interest in Carsons, a Glasgow firm. In 1913 Packers opened another new factory, this time about five miles to the north at Shortwood, and it was to there that Carsons was relocated.

Unfortunately, the depression of the 1930s put a great strain upon the company's finances and in spite of selling off its large and locally famous playing fields and pavilion, as well as the houses owned by the firm, it was still found necessary to cut the factory workers wages from £3 12s per week down to £3 6s 6d. World War Two, however, brought about a return to stability for Packers, but this was to be relatively short lived as, by the 1950s, the financial problems returned, preventing any new investment from being made in any new machinery. By the end of the decade the situation was not looking very bright for the company's 1,100 or so employees, and in 1961 the firm was forced to sell the Shortwood factory and to transfer the Carson's production to Greenbank.

The firm's days of independence were by then

James Goldsmith, who subsequently formed Cavenham Confectionary. During the next two years both Yeatmans of London and Paramount Laboratories were purchased by the new concern, and their production of sweet cigarettes transferred to the Greenbank factory. This was followed in 1968 by the acquisition of the Elizabeth Shaw brand name and the recipes for the famous mint crisp chocolates, the manufacturing of which was soon transferred from Camberley to Bristol. Finally, in 1972, Lindt awarded the firm a contract to produce a range of Easter Eggs and other novelties, for which new production facilities had to be installed.

Cavenhams connection with Greenbank ended in 1981 when the undertaking was sold for £8 million to the firm's existing directors, who had been backed by a major financial institution. A new company, Famous Names Ltd, was created, only to be acquired by Imperial Tobacco plc in 1985 and incorporated into Imperial Foods. The takeovers now gathered pace and complexity as the following year Imperial Tobacco themselves were acquired by the Hanson Trust, while Famous Names Ltd were re-titled Elizabeth Shaw Ltd in 1988.

quickly coming to an end, and in 1964 the whole operation, including the Packer, Carson and Bond brands, was sold to the wealthy entrepreneur Sir

Some of the staff of Packers' Greenbank factory pose for a group photograph, *c.*1909.

The Girls' Meal Room at Packers' Greenbank factory, *c*.1909.

An artist impression of Packers' Greenbank factory as it appeared *c*.1909.

The following year the company management bought out Hanson, this time with a little help from LEAF, the Amsterdam-based international confectionery wing of the Finnish Huhtamaki Group, which, during 1990, went on to take complete control of Elizabeth Shaw Ltd. In 1991 the new owners renamed their acquisition LEAF UK Ltd, but in 1999 the LEAF Group in turn was passed on by their Finnish owners to CSM, a Dutch confectionery undertaking.

However, they quickly decided to focus their attention upon the sugar confectionery side of the business, and consequently for the third time in its history the Greenbank factory, together with its

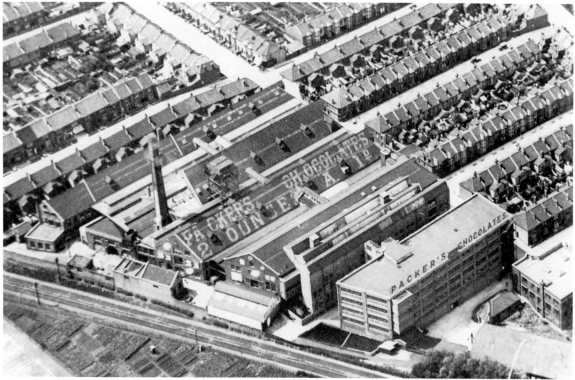

An aerial view of Packers' Greenbank factory during the 1920s.

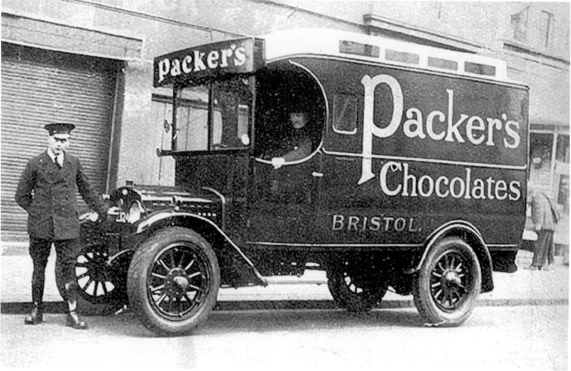

A Packers' delivery van, *c.*1924.

well known Elizabeth Shaw and Famous Names brands, became the object of a management buy out attempt. This was successful, and in March 2000 Packbond Holdings took possession of the company, which was renamed Elizabeth Shaw Ltd, ensuring that the Carlyle Road factory is still continuing Bristol's long and honourable tradition of chocolate manufacturing.

CHAPTER 8
Printing and Packaging

Up until the middle of the 19th century printing in Bristol was still being conducted as a small-scale handicraft industry, its techniques having changed little since its introduction to the city back in 1695. However, after about 1850 the newspaper and book publishing sector started to expand as real incomes rose, literacy spread and the railways demanded large quantities of cheap timetables. At the same time a new market for printed and packaged goods was developing as the manufacturers of mass-produced consumer goods increasingly requested distinctive packaging and promotional material.

Consequently, by the end of the 19th century the printing industry had effectively split itself into four distinct sectors, jobbing printing, book printing, newspaper printing and the manufacturing of stationery and packaging. As the latter had to be carried out on a large scale it was within concerns that specialised in that type of work that the largest number of people came to be employed. Bristol, with factories producing such diverse things as tobacco, chocolate, cocoa, boots, shoes and corsets, soon benefited from the devel-

opment of the packaging sector, and by 1888 seven undertakings in the city are known to have been manufacturing paper bags, two of which went on to become major local employers.

Mardon, Son & Hall

The oldest of these, which for many years was known as Mardon, Son & Hall, can trace its origins back to 1823 when John Price established a small printing business at 12 John Street, Bristol. In 1827 he went into partnership with John Harris who, in 1846, invited his brother-in-law James Mardon to move down from South Molton in Gloucestershire to join the fledgling engraving and printing firm. Harris & Mardon then relocated the short distance to 12 Broad Street, where they initially concentrated on producing headed business notepaper, bill heads, address cards, cheque books and share certificates. Successful though they were with this type of work, it was the decision to concentrate on the printing of packaging materials that was really to transform the business. This began with Harris & Mardon supplying large numbers of pin papers to the

Mardon & Sons' premises in St Stephen's Street, *c*.1860.

chased two second hand presses, which also allowed them to begin printing labels. John Harris's health then began to fail, forcing him to retire from the firm in 1854, leaving James Mardon as the sole proprietor. He continued to build up the business and in 1859 moved it to larger premises in St Stephen's Street, where he diversified into letterpress printing following the installation of some second hand steam-powered presses. The company was then able to advertise as 'Engravers, Lithographers and General Printers by Steam Power.'

Quaker Robert Charlton, who owned a large pin manufactory in Two Mile Hill, Kingswood, and soon the partners were commissioned to print the tobacco wrappers for the local firm of Franklin, Davey & Company.

By the middle of the 19th century the first mechanised lithographic presses had begun to appear, and as these allowed multiple copies to be printed side by side on a single large sheet they were ideal for the production of packaging material. Harris & Mardon were quick to realise the potential of lithography, and in 1849 they pur-

In 1860 James's son, Heber Mardon, became a partner in the company, and three years later his brother-in-law George Hall joined the firm, which was then retitled Mardon, Son & Hall. There then followed a period of sustained expansion, largely due to the efforts of Heber, whose enthusiasm for the most modern machinery and production techniques ensured that the company prospered throughout the latter part of the 19th century.

A worker at Mardon, Son & Hall checks the quality of the printing on 'Player's Navy Cut' cigarette packets in 1950.

Mardon, Son & Hall's Caxton Works (No.1 Factory) at Temple Gate was destroyed by enemy action during the evening of 24 November 1940.

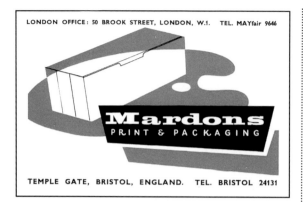

A six-colour Roland Ultra sheet-fed litho press in Mardons' No.11 factory at St Anne's.

During the 1860s Mardons began branching out by acquiring an interest in paper mills in Pensford and Bath, while in 1866 work began on a completely new four-storey factory in Milk Street, to which production was finally transferred in 1869. Here they went on to become the first undertaking in Bristol to manufacture cardboard boxes, and were soon supplying these to a variety of local firms, including makers of collars, corsets, boots and shoes, drapery and tailoring. Good though this trade was, the real turning point came in 1888 when Mardons began to print the packets for Wills cigarettes. Within a short time they became 'to a great extent the printers for the tobacco trade in England', and as such their future was assured.

In fact, business then grew so rapidly that extra premises were acquired in Rupert Street and Dighton Street, while in 1894 it was found necessary to open a huge new factory at Temple Gate, later known as No.1 Factory, and in 1897 No.2 Factory nearby in Temple Street, exclusively for lithography and the highly specialised facsimile printing process of Collotype.

The new century opened with the American Tobacco Company attempting a full-scale assault on the British market, to which UK manufacturers responded by forming themselves into Imperial Tobacco (of Great Britain and Ireland) Ltd in October 1901. No sooner had this been created than the new consortium began negotiations with Mardons to prevent a number of its patents for packaging machines from falling into American hands. Consequently, in 1902 Mardon, Son & Hall became part of Imperial Tobacco. This, however, did nothing to slow down Mardons' expansion and eight new factories went on line between 1902 and 1915, with the number rising to 11 with the opening of St Anne's in 1922. Three years later Heber Mardon died, but the undertaking he had done so much to develop continued to flourish, ensuring that the name Mardon, Son & Hall Ltd, as it became in 1938, remained in use until the latter part of the 20th century.

As with so many of the other great local entrepreneurs, the Mardons were nonconformists and wedded to the philosophy of benevolent paternalism in dealings with its employees. From its formation days the company realised the importance of good industrial relations, and as early as the 1850s Mardons granted their employees a half-holiday on Saturdays, something totally new in the printing trade. With working conditions matched in Bristol only by Fry's, Robinsons or Wills, recruitment was easy, worker numbers rising from just 200 in the 1880s, to 3,800 by 1915 and 5,270 by the end of the 1930s, by which time Mardons was one of the largest printing establishments in the world.

which did so much to provide generations of Bristolians with well paid and secure employment.

The winter of 1940–41 was to prove the most turbulent in the company's history, as during the course of German air attacks on Bristol Mardons had the misfortune of losing 10 of its 13 factories and warehouses around Temple Gate. This was the largest loss suffered by any company in the city. Fortunately, printing houses large and small, both locally and in other parts of the country, rallied round and gave assistance to aid the remarkable recovery that was made later in 1941. After the war Mardons was able to rebuild and expand, and by 1979, when the 19th factory opened, they had premises dedicated to turning out printed paper and board being sprawled across the Bristol area from York Road and Winterstoke Road to Temple Gate, St Anne's, Brislington and Warmley.

In March 1989 the group was renamed LMG Mardon in order to reflect its acquisition by Lawson, a Canadian packaging group, and during the next 20 or so years the whole local operation was consolidated. Consequently, today Lawson-Mardon Packaging Ltd, which has been owned by Alcan Inc. of Canada since 2001, operates exclusively from the Tower Road North site at Warmley, the direct descendent of a company

The English Corrugating Paper Company

As a result of Mardon, Son & Hall becoming part of Imperial Tobacco, John Mardon, one of James Mardon's sons, decided to branch out on his own, and in 1908 founded The English Corrugating Paper Company in Portland Square, St Paul's. At that time corrugated paper was a relatively new packaging medium, and as off the shelf machines for its production were not readily available John Mardon built his own, a tradition continued by his son Kenneth and his two grandsons until the 1960s when modern technology rendered this activity redundant.

Meanwhile, during the 1920s the firm set up a new factory close by in Wilson Place, while in 1924 John Mardon's son, Kenneth, joined the company, and it was he who extended its product range into making rigid corrugated packaging such as boxes and boards, and converted the undertaking into a limited company. Kenneth Mardon was still Chairman and Managing

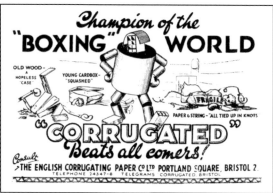

Director of The English Corrugating Paper Company at the time of his death in 1973, after which the firm passed into the hands of his sons, Bernard, who died in 1971, John and Bruce. The latter was serving as Chairman in 1989. A booklet featuring many of their classic advertisements from the 1920s and 30s was published by popular demand!

Today the company is still owned by descendants of its founder, and although both John and Bruce Mardon passed away in 2000, two of John Mardon's great-grandsons, David Thornton and Christopher Mardon, are currently joint managing directors. They are carrying on the family tradition of developing the firm to satisfy customer and market demands for corrugated packaging. Today, the company, which currently employs some 65 people, prides itself on being able to offer a complete in-house production service through from sheet manufacture, design and die cutting to overprinting and conversion into a limitless variety of boxes, cases, cartons and fitments, thereby demonstrating that a long-estab-

lished, family- run concern can still successfully adapt to meet the challenging requirements of the 21st century.

E.S. & A. Robinson

The other great Bristol packaging undertaking to be established during the 19th century was E.S. & A. Robinson, but unlike Mardon, Son & Hall, which began life in the traditional printing sector, Robinsons were involved with packaging from the very beginning. Its founder was Elisha Smith Robinson, a native of Overbury near Tewkesbury, where his father was the proprietor of a paper mill. After being sent away to serve his apprenticeship the young Elisa could not settle back in the family firm, and so he decided to move to Bristol with the intention of establishing himself in the newly emerging packaging industry. While work-

THINGS WORTH SEEING AT
E. S. & A. ROBINSON'S
Paper & Paper Bag Warehouse,
2, REDCLIFF STREET,
BRISTOL.

TWO LITHOGRAPHIC PRINTING OFFICES,
One Seventy-five feet long, the other, Sixty-five feet long, containing Twenty Lithographic Presses and four Lithographic MACHINES, worked by steam power, perfectly unique and peculiar to this Establishment, doing as much work as Forty presses, and executing the work with greater precision than can be attained by hand labour; machine also for cutting and glazing paper.

50,000 Reams of the most useful Sizes in
BROWN AND SHOP PAPER,
AND A LARGER
ASSORTMENT OF PAPER BAGS
than any other house in Great Britain.
A PAGING MACHINE
Capable of numbering, consecutively or alternately, from 1 to 999,000

COPPER PLATE PRINTING.
LETTER-PRESS PRINTING.

Direction Labels, Machine Ruling, and Gold Lettering.
CUTTING, by Wilson's Patent, and other Machines, by Steam Power.
All the latest Designs for Tea and Tobacco Papers, either in Lithograph or Letter-Press.
Numerous and varied forms and patterns of
Invoice Heads, Circulars, Cards, Cheque, Receipt, and Order Books,
Plain and Ornamental.
ILLUSTRATIVE ENGRAVINGS
Of the best Colours, done on the Premises.

ing in his grandfather's general store in the Cotswold village of Blockley, he had already noticed the way in which each customer's purchases were wrapped using single sheets of paper

and in particular the skill necessary to make the 'twists' that held such things as sugar, tea and flour. There had to be a better way, and the answer to Elisha seemed to be to use ready-made paper bags, and it was these he set out to supply.

The new business was launched in 1844 with a capital of £190, over half of which was borrowed, and during the first year of trading a profit of £400 was made on the handmade bags supplied to the grocery trade. The business was soon flourishing, and in 1846 E.S. Robinson was able to move to larger premises nearby at 2 Redcliff Street, where he traded as a 'Paper Merchant and Grocer's Stationer'. Two years later his younger brother Alfred came to join him, and soon the firm was trading as E.S. & A. Robinson and in 1850 they acquired a hand lithographic press that allowed them to print advertisements, illustrations and the trader's name onto the bags and wrapping paper. In 1856 this process was mechanised and in 1860 the first bag-making machine was purchased.

By modern standards work in the factory was hard and the hours almost inhumanly long. In the early 1870s the men began work at six in the morning, and although this was later put back to eight o'clock they were still expected to toil through until seven in the evening. Nevertheless, in the weeks leading up to Christmas overtime, almost enthusiastically looked forward to for its reward, went on till 9.30pm. In 1858 a half-day holiday was granted but apart from public holidays there were no others, except for the annual firm's outing on a July Saturday.

Elisha and Alfred Robinson soon found themselves proprietors of a thriving business, and by astutely ploughing back much of the profits they were able to further expand and diversify. Consequently, in 1873 Elisha acquired the British rights for a high speed American machine able to produce unique satchel-shaped paper bags incorporating a gusset, something essential if they were to be mechanically filled by the customer. Following the introduction of these cheap machine-made bags the company's success was assured, requiring them to expand their premises along Redcliff Street before taking over the corner block of Redcliff Street and Victoria Street, where a fine large building in the 'Bristol Byzantine' style was opened in 1878.

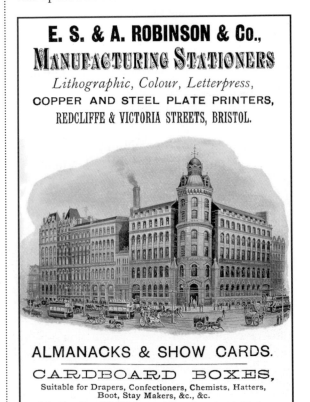

E.S. & A. Robinson's administration block, which stood at the corner of Victoria Street and Redcliff Street. It was built in 1903 after the previous building on the site had been destroyed by fire. This was severely damaged by enemy action during 1941, as can be seen in this photograph, and, consequently, was demolished in 1961 to be replaced by a new 15-storey office block, Bristol's first skyscraper.

The manufacture of paper bags by E.S. & A. Robinson.

By that time the technological revolution in the
printing trade was gathering pace, and during the
1870s Robinsons bought the printing works of
Ensor & Company in Marsh Street where they
installed new colour lithography equipment to
produce calendars and trade almanacs over-
printed with the name and address of the customer. These also proved to be very popular, and
by 1882 E.S. & A. Robinson were producing some
685,000 almanacs annually, all in full colour,
encouraging them to transfer the colour printing
to fine new buildings in Bedminster, which were
opened in 1887.

Elisha Robinson was a staunch Baptist who
played a considerable part in the building of
Tyndale Baptist Chapel. In addition, he was a lifelong Liberal who not only served as a local Justice
of the Peace but also became Mayor of Bristol in
1866 and was, for many years, chairman of the
Port and Pier Railway and a consistent supporter
of the Avonmouth Dock scheme. He was remembered by many of the workers as a kindly jovial
sort of man who made it his business to walk

around the factory at Christmas distributing
small gifts to his employees.

Consequently, Robinsons seems to have been
an harmonious place in which to work, prompting a visitor to remark in 1883 that 'wherever we
went, we noticed that the hands, both male and
female, seemed to be of a superior class, and that
they are evidently well satisfied and contented.' It
was also noted that 'In the course of a year, every
employee has a week's paid holiday, and there is a
capital system of time rewards, whereby everyone
in the service of the house earning over 10
shillings a week is entitled to a sovereign at mid-
summer, 3d being deducted for each late arrival.
This is an excellent and practical method of stim-
ulating punctuality, and this scheme and holidays
cost the firm nearly £1,500 per annum.'

Changes, however, were soon afoot, and in
1885 Elisha Robinson died, after which his sons,
Edward, who had started with the company in
1869, and Arthur, who had joined in 1874, took
control, and when Alfred finally retired in 1893
they reorganised E.S. & A. Robinson as a limited
company. Over the next 20 years expansion continued unabated, starting in 1887 when the decision was made to build the spacious new factory
at East Street, Bedminster. Two years later a week's
holiday with pay was introduced for all those having 12 months' service, something almost
unknown at the time, while not long after Edward
Robinson made a personal gift of £5,000 as a
nucleus of a pension fund. During the late 19th
century the technique for manufacturing folding
boxes was discovered by an American, and

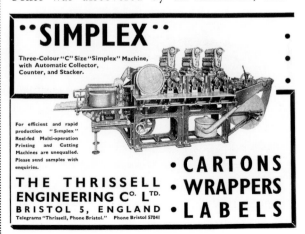

Thrissell Engineering's Easton Road works, photographed during the 1930s.

E.S. & A. Robinson's cardboard box factory in Filwood Road, Fishponds, shortly after opening in 1922.

Robinsons soon established a special department for the purpose at Bedminster. The demand for the cartons grew steadily and later, in 1922, a specially built one-floor factory devoted solely to their production was opened at Fishponds. Likewise, the 'Rigid' box business also increased rapidly, necessitating a move to a larger building in St Philip's.

By the early 1890s Robinsons were employing some 800 people, and between 1890 and 1903 nine new buildings were constructed, while a disastrous fire at Redcliff Street, also in 1903, gave the firm the opportunity to modernise. In 1908 offset lithography was introduced and the working week reduced to 50 hours, while 1912 saw the opening of the new Malago paper bag factory in

In 1929 Robinsons built a waxed paper factory in Filwood Road, Fishponds, and over the years it was enlarged several times. This photograph, taken in 1958, shows a newly erected frontage.

Bedminster's Argus Road, a facility with an initial capacity of 11 million bags a week. This ferro-concrete building boasted a recreation ground on the roof and during the summer it was arranged that work should start earlier in order that sports might be played in the evening at the firm's own athletic ground. By that time the company had factories covering 10 and a half acres, while before World War One finally broke out the 2,500 employees were also benefiting from a profit-sharing scheme and free medical and dental treatment.

By the end of the conflict the next generation of Robinsons, Foster, Harold, and Colonel Percy, were already making their marks on the business, although Edward, their father, remained chairman until 1929. An example of this was the introduction of cellophane bags, something for which Foster Robinson was largely responsible. These were manufactured at the Malago factory where the American 'Colodense' process for printing on cellophane was also adopted. In addition to the tried and trusted method of internally funding their growth, during the post war period the company also embarked upon a policy of acquiring a number of subsidiary companies, all of which were involved in some way with the manufacturing of paper or its related products.

As a result Strachan & Henshaw, the Bristol engineering firm established in 1879, which produced the bag manufacturing machines for Robinsons, was taken over in 1920, after which they went on to become a market leader in the production of machinery for the printing and packaging trades. Although not owned by Robinsons, another local engineering firm, the Thrissell Engineering Company, which could trace its origins back to 1805, also produced a wide range of machines for the box-making, printing and packaging industry at its Easton Road factory, and it survived right through until 1982, by which time it was part of the Masson Scott Thrissell Group.

During the 1920s Robinsons also obtained the licence to manufacture strong and economic multi-wall paper sacks. These soon became a popular carrier for lime and cement due to the incorporation of a self-closing valve that obviated the necessity for tying when the sacks were being filled by automatic weighing and filling machines. To produce these, Robinsons formed a subsidiary company known as Paper Sacks Ltd.,

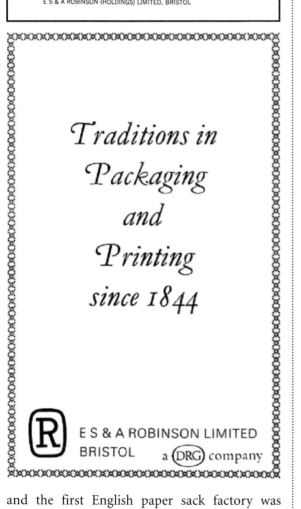
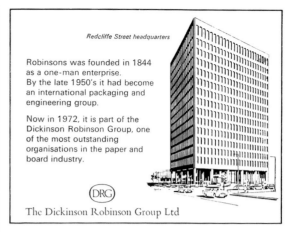
paper sack business moved to that home of cement at Northfleet.

A further move to Keynsham took place in 1932 when Robinsons built a paper mill on what seemed a perfect site, close to Bristol docks and railway, with unlimited water power at hand and in the midst of the Somerset coalfield. This was operated as Keynsham Paper Mills Ltd, also run as a subsidiary company of E.S. & A. Robinson. Another innovation was waxed paper, the first machines for its production being set up in the Malago factory in 1924. However, demand for this hygienic wrapping, which was initially used to package bread and such like, grew so rapidly that in 1929 its manufacture was moved to a fine new factory in Filwood Road, Fishponds, which in due course became the Robinson Waxed Paper Company, yet another subsidiary undertaking.

After World War Two Robinsons continued to prosper, by which time it had become the most important of its kind in Britain, and after the conflict it continued its development by introducing new packaging products such as sterile packs for medicine and surgical supplies and foil packets for Polaroid film cassettes. This led, in 1960, to the formation of E.S. & A. Robinson (Holdings) Ltd., which in 1965 built Bristol's first skyscraper on the site of their old office by Bristol Bridge.

This new headquarters building was the last true Robinson project as in 1966, by which time no member of the founding family was engaged in senior management, the shareholders agreed a merger with the Hemel Hempstead firm John

and the first English paper sack factory was opened in Bristol. In 1927 they took over a new site at Keynsham, but three years later the factory there was given over to another purpose and the

Basildon Bond
Sellotape
REGD. TRADE MARK

Croxley TRANSCRIPT

Three Candlesticks

Giant Manilla
QUEEN'S VELVET
Challenge
LION BRAND
Croxley Script

We've made names for ourselves...

with *Basildon Bond, Sellotape* and the many other leading domestic and commercial brands manufactured by Dickinson Robinson Group companies and marketed in many parts of the world.

...in packaging too.

But DRG expertise does not end there. We are equally active and successful in the field of packaging where our materials, processes, printing facilities and systems technology are used in the production of packs which variously protect, preserve and promote the well known brands of our customers in the food, drinks, household, cosmetics, fashion, medical and many other markets. Much of this packaging is produced in Bristol, where we also have specialised engineering companies.

(DRG) The Dickinson Robinson Group Ltd
1 Redcliffe Street, Bristol BS99 7QY   Telephone 0272 294294
ENVELOPES : STATIONERY : PACKAGING : SELF-ADHESIVE PRODUCTS : SPECIALISED ENGINEERING

Dickinson & Company Ltd. This produced the Dickinson Robinson Group (DRG), which contained the two largest printing and stationary companies in the country, with holdings in South Africa, Australia, New Zealand, Canada, the US and Europe.

However, by the 1980s all was not well as the poor economic climate, the arrival of new competition and the expiry of a number of the group's important patents had all conspired to slash profits, and in 1989 the Pembridge Group, later known as Redcliff Investments, acquired a majority shareholding. Their plan was to realise the asset value of the undertaking through restructuring and the sale of certain parts. Consequently, the various local components were disbursed and came into the hands of a variety of owners including Bowater Industries, the Weir Group and Credit Lyonnais, and today the carton factory in Filwood Road, Fishponds, is operated by Graphic Packaging.

Likewise, the waxed paper factory, RWP Robinson, also in Filwood Road, left the DRG Group to become Rexam Custom, and at the beginning of 1996 it still employed about 125 people producing packaging material. However, in April of that year 55 staff were made redundant

Robinsons' old East Street factory still acts as a landmark in the Bedminster area, and the lettering 'E.S. & A. Robinson Ltd Paper Bag Makers' and 'E.S. & A. Robinson Ltd Colour Printers' is still visible on the building reminding local people of what was once one of the area's major employers.

Robinsons' old waxed paper factory in Filwood Road, Fishponds. Now known as Verona House, its main occupier is currently Zanetti & Bailey, the marble floor specialists.

when that operation shut down. The works then turned to making coated photographic and film products but, after failing to win enough customers to keep going, closed later in the year with the loss of 80 more jobs, and today the building, now known as Verona House, is home to several different companies.

St Anne's Board Mills during the 1950s.

St Anne's Board Mills

The early years of the 20th century witnessed a growing demand for paperboard which, being much stronger than the paper, was steadily taking over as the material of choice for packaging cigarettes. This led to Imperial Tobacco and the British-American Tobacco Company deciding to establish their own board mill on a nine-acre site on the south bank of the River Avon at St Anne's. Here was to be found the plentiful supply of water necessary for the production process, while coal and wood pulp could both be brought in by barge.

The St Anne's Board Mill Company was incorporated on 2 July 1913, Mr G.H. Hedley, who owned a board mill at Loudwater in Buckinghamshire, being appointed its first manager. Paperboard production began in November of the following year and during 1915, its first full year on line, some 3,496 tons were produced using just one machine. A second was installed in

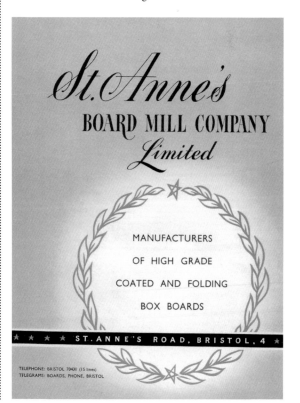

An aerial view of St Anne's Board Mills.

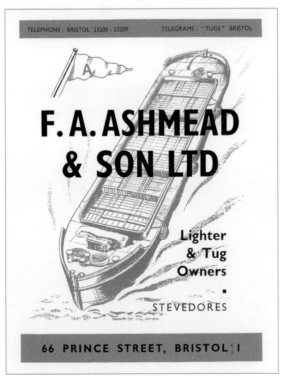

interest in the new mill, as well as its subsidiary, G.H. Headley Ltd, which then became totally owned by Imperial Tobacco. In 1922 they installed a third machine and the following year production had reached 12,998 tons, while the purchase of a further three machines during the 1930s ensured that output had risen to 70,365 by the time World War Two broke out. During the conflict the machines were kept running as far as conditions would allow for up to 168 hours a week, and as the call-up reduced the number of people employed in the mill those remaining had to work 12-hour shifts.

A pressing need arose for packages that would protect stores during campaigns in the tropics, and St Anne's Board Mill Company Ltd was largely responsible for producing a container board incorporating a large proportion of pitch. As it was found to completely resist water penetration and repelled termites, thousands of tons were ordered for the armed forces.

When the war finally ended, a programme of machine reconstruction was initiated, and by 1958 production was topping 100,000 tons per

October 1917 and this enabled 8,879 tons of board to be manufactured during 1919.

After World War One had ended, Imperial acquired the British-American Tobacco Company's

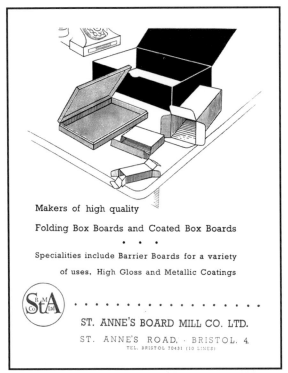

Makers of high quality

Folding Box Boards and Coated Box Boards

• • •

Specialities include Barrier Boards for a variety

of uses, High Gloss and Metallic Coatings

ST. ANNE'S BOARD MILL CO. LTD.

ST. ANNE'S ROAD. · BRISTOL. 4.

TEL. BRISTOL 70431 (10 LINES)

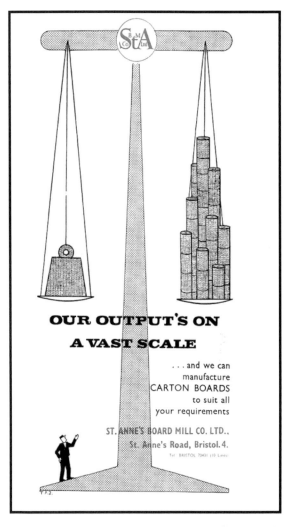

OUR OUTPUT'S ON

A VAST SCALE

. . . and we can
manufacture
CARTON BOARDS
to suit all
your requirements

ST. ANNE'S BOARD MILL CO. LTD.,
St. Anne's Road, Bristol. 4.

Tel. BRISTOL 70431 (10 Lines)

This photograph shows how important the River Avon was for transporting the raw materials to St Anne's Board Mills.

annum, with the plant, which by then was covering over 100 acres, turning out an average of 14 tons per hour. For many years wood pulp from Scandinavia was the principal commodity at the Bristol City Docks, from where it was transported to St Anne's Board Mills by F.A. Ashmead's barges, each of which was towed from the City Docks by way of the Feeder Canal. However, by the late 1960s it had already been decided to close the City Docks, and although in 1970 a new wood pulp terminal was constructed at Portishead, by that time St Anne's output was far exceeding the requirements of the declining tobacco industry.

Even though alternative markets were found,

with about half the plant's production eventually being used for packaging chocolates, pharmaceutical products, cereals and other foodstuffs, competition from foreign rivals, which benefited from heavy fuel subsidies, increased dramatically. The availability of more home-produced pulp, coupled with the decline of St Anne's Board Mill, led to the premature closure of the new wood pulp terminal in 1976, while the Board Mills themselves ceased production in October 1980. This caused some 1,700 people to lose their jobs, and between 1982 and 1984 the old manufacturing complex was completely demolished and the whole site cleared for redevelopment.

Ashton Containers

Another totally owned subsidiary of Imperial Tobacco was Ashton Containers, an undertaking originally formed in 1919. At that time it was known as Ashton Saw Mills Ltd. and had been set up in order to supply timber for Imperial's packing case factory, an undertaking which transferred to Ashton Gate in 1921. The firm's name was changed to Ashton Containers in 1937, as by then it had switched to the manufacture of fibreboard containers and packing cases, and although by 1954 some 41 percent of the company's trade was still with Imperial, 17 percent was with other tobacco manufacturers and 42 percent with customers in other trades. Following the closure of St Anne's Board Mills, Imperial sought a buyer for Ashton Containers, and in 1983 the Winterstoke Road operation was acquired by the St Regis Paper Company, which in turn became part of David S. Smith (Holdings) plc in 1986. As a result, in 1988 production was moved to a new site at Royal Portbury Dock, where today it operates as D.S. Smith Corrugated Bristol.

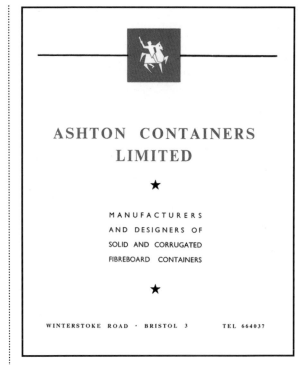

ASHTON CONTAINERS LIMITED

★

MANUFACTURERS AND DESIGNERS OF SOLID AND CORRUGATED FIBREBOARD CONTAINERS

★

WINTERSTOKE ROAD · BRISTOL 3   TEL 664037

CHAPTER 9
Ships, Locomotives, Carriages and Wagons

One important result of diverting the course of the River Frome in the mid-13th century was that the Marsh, a valuable area of open land, better known today as Queen Square, was added to the city, and it was there that shipbuilding soon became established. Such work continued to be carried out on the Marsh until around 1700 when land reclamation and the laying out of Queen Square conspired to force Bristol's shipbuilders to move further down the River Avon, and by the mid-18th century this work was being carried out at various points on both banks between Wapping and Jacob's Wells.

So skilfully and thoroughly was this work carried out that throughout the world the phrase 'Ship Shape and Bristol Fashion' was soon being applied to vessels constructed from high quality Forest of Dean oak by the city's shipwrights, thus establishing a tradition for quality and craftsmanship in manufacturing that has lasted right up until the present day. In order to oversee the construction of their vessels, Bristol ship owners generally preferred to have them built locally, and this in time led some to make heavy investments in a chosen yard, or to actually build the ships themselves.

Charles Hill & Son Ltd

Typical of the owners turned builders were the Hilhouse family who, after being ship owners for some two generations, finally branched out into construction, and in so doing laid the foundations

A typical 18th-century Bristol shipyard. This drawing depicts Sydenham Teast's at Wapping in about 1760.

WAR OFFICE STEAM PACKETS.

BRISTOL, DUBLIN, CORK,

and TENBY.

THE War Office Steam Packet *GEORGE IV.* JOHN BROWN, Commander, Sails from BRISTOL for CORK every SATURDAY, and leaves CORK for BRISTOL every TUESDAY.

The War Office Steam Packet *PALMERSTON*, JOHN HYDE, Commander, Sails from BRISTOL for DUBLIN every WEDNESDAY, and leaves DUBLIN for BRISTOL every SATURDAY.

These Steam Packets are built entirely of Oak, from the identical Models and Plans of the Royal Sovereign and Meteor Holyhead Post-Office Steam Packets (which from their superior construction have continued their voyages regularly through the whole winter.) They are completed with entirely new Engines of the best and most approved principles; their accommodations are arranged in Separate Cabins.

War Office Steam Packet Office, Bristol, June, 1823.

of what became Bristol's most important and long lasting firm of shipbuilders. It all began in about 1770 when the young James Martin Hilhouse began shipbuilding in a new yard conveniently situated in Hotwell Road, adjacent to what was soon to be known as the Merchant's Dock. He probably launched his first ship in 1773 and between 1778 and 1786 was fortunate to obtain orders for 12 others from the Admiralty, one of these being the 'Nassau' which, at 1,384 tons, was the largest vessel yet built in Bristol. This work really established James Hilhouse's reputation, and after this he turned his attention to the construction of merchantmen, a number of which were destined for the West Indies run.

The year 1803 saw the business retitled Hilhouse & Sons and Company, and exactly 10 years later they completed the 'Charlotte and Hope', which although only intended for use in the docks was nevertheless the first steamship ever to be built in Bristol. This pioneering work led to the firm being given an order by the newly formed War Office Steam Packet Company to build the 'George IV' and the 'Palmerston', two large wooden paddle steamers for use on the Bristol to Cork run, both of which were launched in 1822.

Meanwhile, the creation of the Floating

Hilhouse & Son's newly opened yard at Mardyke as it appeared in 1826. To the rear can be seen Sydney Row, built specially to house the workers. The undertaking later became known as the Albion Dockyard.

The launch of the 'New York City' from Charles Hill's Albion Dockyard on 16 July 1917.

Harbour led Hilhouse & Sons and Company to shift its attention to the south bank of the river opposite Mardyke where they laid out their New Dockyard, which also boasted a dry-dock. The first ship, a West Indiaman, was launched from there in 1820, allowing the firm to close the Hotwells site in 1823. The following year the firm was re-titled George Hilhouse & Company, while in 1825 Charles Hill, who had joined the company in 1810 as an accountant, became a partner in the business, which finally began trading as Hilhouse, Hill & Company in 1839. Soon after, Charles Hill took control of the business and brought in his 16-year-old son, also named Charles, and in 1845 the firm was renamed Charles Hill & Son. Three years later their New Dockyard was retitled the Albion Yard, a name still used by David Abels, the boat builder, whose business occupies the site today.

However, in spite of some Bristol shipbuilders being eager to embrace new technology they were unable to obtain the large amounts of iron plates and girders required as cheaply as their northern rivals. To further add to their problems, the River

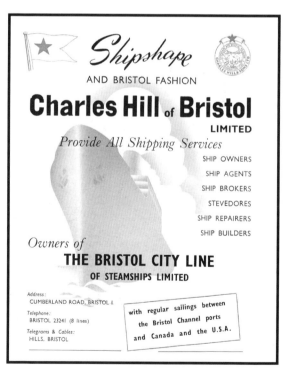

Avon restricted the size of vessels that could be built to around 3,000 tons, something which became an increasing disadvantage as the demand for larger ships rapidly increased. Nevertheless, the firm persevered and continued building

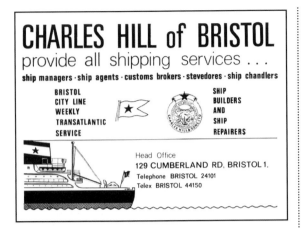

medium-sized vessels of between 300 and 400 tons for trade, while before Charles Hill senior died in 1866 the yard had also begun making a good profit from repairing badly damaged ships and then buying them up.

Great changes in shipbuilding were now taking place, and in 1881 Charles Hill's shipyard laid down their first iron ship, the 247 ton steam collier 'Valeria'. The 'Wells City', a 1,814 ton ship for the Bristol City Line, followed in 1890, while five years later Hills launched their last large sailing vessel, the 1,363 ton barque 'Favell'. Although Charles Hill junior died in 1900 and the early years of the 20th century were marked by depression, by the time World War One broke out Hills had become established as the principal shipbuilders and repairers in Bristol.

A view across the harbour to Charles Hill's Albion Dockyard. This photograph was taken during the late 1930s.

Charles Hill's Albion Dockyard as it appeared in 1970.

During the conflict they were called upon to build more ships than ever before, and between 1914 and 1919 they constructed eight standard steamships for the Shipping Controller. This type of work also continued after the war, and between

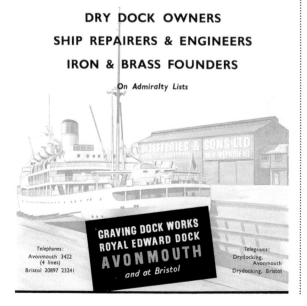
1920 and 1923 some 12 vessels of over 1,800 tons were launched to replace wartime losses, and one of these was the 3,554 ton steamship 'Neptuna', the largest vessel ever built in Bristol. During the remainder of the 1920s, and right through until the outbreak of World War Two, the company survived by specialising in building smaller vessels, with nearly a hundred barges, tugs, hoppers, tankers and other small craft of between 18 and 800 tons being constructed in Hills' four building berths.

With war clouds appearing once more on the horizon, Charles Hill & Son again started to receive Government contracts, and between 1938 and 1946 the firm's contribution to the war effort amounted to four boom defence vessels; eight Flower class corvettes; seven River class frigates; six Loch class frigates; one large LCT; 13 small LCM's and four water-carrying vessels. Some 2,000 vessels were also repaired and refitted, and it was during the war years that Hills officially adopted the centuries old 'Shipshape and Bristol fashion' motto. In 1946 Charles Hill & Son Ltd took over the Great Western Steamship Company's old dockyard next door to them, which after being put to a variety of uses had, in

The launching of the 1,541 ton *Miranda Guinness* at the Albion Dockyard on 9 July 1976. She was the last large ship ever to be built in Bristol.

1902, been purchased by the city council and turned into the Corporation Commercial Dry Dock.

Once the war was behind them, Hills went back to building small specialised vessels such as tugs, dredgers, ferries and tankers, and during the 1950s they became a public company. The firm was then at its most diverse, owning, among others, such well-known local concerns as Jefferies Avonmouth Ltd, the ship repairers and engineers, Reed, Stock & Company Ltd, Stevedores and Nott Brodie & Company Ltd, civil engineers and building contractors.

However, the announcement made in 1970 that commercial operations in the Bristol City Docks were soon to cease effectively put an end to local shipbuilding.

Consequently, the 1,541 ton *Miranda Guinness*, which was launched by Hills on 9 July 1976, was the last ship ever to be built in Bristol, while the closure of the Albion Dockyard on 4 January 1977 marked it as the day on which another of Bristol's traditional industries passed into history.

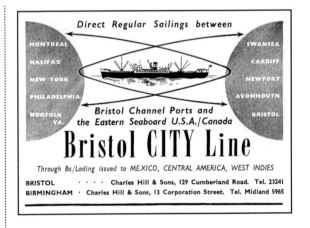

The Bristol City Line

As Bristol lost ground as a shipbuilding centre during the 1840s, Charles Hill & Son began diversifying, and assembled a fleet of old sailing ships for use on the West Indies routes. However, by 1856 world trade patterns had changed, and in order to move with the times Hills sold off all their small West Indies boats and invested in two very large ships to carry both cargo and passengers to the newly opened lands of India and Australia. This proved to be a shrewd move, and by 1872 Charles Hill junior owned 18 vessels, while in 1879 he founded the Bristol City Line, which ran steamships to New York in competition with the Great Western Steamship Line.

Unlike its rival, the Bristol City Line carried cargo rather than passengers and was based in the Bristol City Docks rather than at Avonmouth, and so successful were they that in 1884 they had forced the Great Western Steamship Line to cease sailing to New York. Finally, in 1887 the Great Western Steamship Company Ltd made its last passenger voyage, after which it switched to being a cargo only operation, before being wound up in 1895.

In contrast, by the turn of the century Hill's had 10 steamships operating on the New York run, and in 1933 a service to Quebec and Montreal was introduced, a route which was extended to the Great Lakes in 1958 when the St Lawrence Seaway opened. The Bristol City Line's trade with North America continued until early February 1972, when, following the Bibby Line of Liverpool's acquisition of a controlling interest in the undertaking, the new owners saw fit to terminate the Bristol - Eastern Seaboard operation.

G.K. Stothert & Company

Another local undertaking involved in shipbuilding in Bristol was the engineering firm Stothert & Slaughter, later G.K. Stothert & Co, and although they constructed over 50 small iron vessels between 1851 and 1904 it is for their work with another form of transport that they are probably best remembered.

In 1837 Henry Asprey Stothert, son of George

A view of G.K. Stothert's Hotwells Shipyard as it appeared during the late 19th century. Unfortunately, this drawing displays a fair degree of artistic license.

Stothert, a Bath ironmonger and foundry owner, went into partnership with his brother John and two Bristol marine engineers, Robert Bruce and George Lander, for 'the establishment of a manufactory of locomotive engines as well as iron machinery of all descriptions'. The site chosen in Bristol was at Cuckold's Pill, later renamed Avonside Wharf, conveniently sited between the terminus of the Bristol & Gloucestershire Railway that brought coal into the city and the Floating Harbour. At that time the whole country was in

the grip of railway mania, and with the construction of both the Great Western Railway and the Bristol & Exeter Railway pressing ahead, Stothert was sure that the Avonside works would be in a strong position to win orders. To ensure that the new firm had the best possible start, in 1839 Stothert enticed away the G.W.R.'s brilliant young assistant engineer Edward Slaughter and appointed him managing partner of the company. At the same time the original partnership was dissolved and the firm re-titled Stothert, Slaughter & Company.

Stotherts' confidence was soon rewarded by a contract for two 'Firefly' class locomotives for the G.W.R., these being delivered just prior to the opening of the railway's Bristol to Bath section in August 1840. Further orders followed from the G.W.R. as the firm quickly established a reputation for quality work at low prices, and between 1841 and 1856 an average of 22 locomotives per year were manufactured by the Avonside Ironworks. By then Edward Slaughter had become the leading figure in local locomotive industry, and his position within the business was further strengthened when Henry Stothert retired in 1852.

At times when locomotive demand was slack, the firm undertook work in the maritime field, manufacturing such things as components for Brunel's 'Great Western', as well as steam pumps and marine engines. In 1844 the principal shareholders, Henry Stothert, Edward Slaughter, John Stothert, Robert Bruce and George Fuller, decided to build and run two 105 ton iron screw steamers across the River Severn between Bristol and Newport, in direct competition with the paddle steamers operated by the Bristol General Steam Navigation Company. In spite of some accidents the project was a success, and the following year John Stothert, Robert Bruce and George Fuller established the New Steam Packet Company, which went on to run their vessels for many years.

In 1852 Stotherts took over the existing Hotwell Yard from its owners, George Lunell & Company, and two years later Stothert & Fripp was set up as a separate shipbuilding concern. The company, which was re-titled George Kelston Stothert in 1857, Stothert and Martin in 1859 and finally G.K. Stothert & Company in 1865, operated what they called the Clifton Marine Engineering and Iron Ship Building Works, and this maintained a reasonably steady output of small vessels until the late 1880s. Sadly, towards the end of the 19th century orders fell off dramatically and the last ship was launched by Stotherts in 1904. After that the firm relied upon repairs and rebuilding work until they were forced to close, the plant finally being sold off in February 1933.

The Avonside Engineering Company

During the 1850s the locomotive side of the market became more secure, and in 1856 the engineer Henry Grüning was persuaded to join Edward Slaughter, the new partnership trading as Slaughter, Grüning & Company. However, as time went by the domestic locomotive market started to become much more competitive as the leading railway companies began building their own engines, and the smaller operators were absorbed by the larger concerns. This forced the independent manufacturers to look elsewhere, and fortu-

nately the second half of the 19th century saw the promotion and construction of railways throughout the world, something of which Slaughter was to take full advantage.

The Avonside factory's first export order came in 1847 when six locomotives were supplied to Tuscany, and by the end of the century the company had sent its products as far afield as India, New Zealand, Australia, South Africa, Chile, Brazil, Mexico, Canada, Spain and Portugal. In 1864, by which time the company was employing between 800 and 900 people, it was reconstituted as the Avonside Engineering Company Ltd, of which William Bevan became chairman and Edward Slaughter managing director, at a salary of £1,200 per annum plus bonuses.

In spite of the opportunities offered by the export market, the 1870s were to prove a difficult time for locomotive builders as the price of coal doubled during the first four years of the decade. On top of this, in early 1873 Avonside had agreed

A view inside the Avonside Engine Company's Fishponds works in 1905 showing the erecting and paint shop.

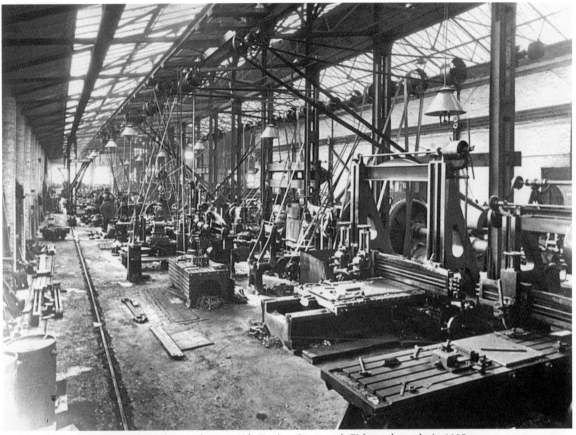

Looking down the main machine shop at the Avonside Engine Company's Fishponds works in 1905.

to adopt the 'nine hour system', and not only was the working week reduced from 58 to 54 hours but shortly after a 6 percent wage increase was implemented. These factors, plus a sharp downturn in home demand, all conspired to increase manufacturing costs, and early in 1878 Avonside announced that wages would have to be cut.

'To the Workmen of the Avonside Engine Company Ltd., Bristol. The Directors very earnestly call your attention to the depression which exists in the locomotive trade generally and more particularly in these works. The result of last year's trading has been most unsatisfactory; instead of earning money the concern has lost heavily… These works cannot be kept open sim-

ply for the benefit of the workpeople at a loss to the shareholders. The Directors have, therefore, after a most careful consideration of the subject, concluded to reduce wages and piece work prices all round, and that this reduction shall be 12 percent.'

This was not well received by the workforce and out of the 800 men employed by the company only 50 were prepared to accept the directors decision. A lockout that lasted for several months resulted and during 1878 lost the company over £7,000. The whole situation had in fact been exacerbated by Edward Slaughter's retirement in 1874, as his replacement, John Lum Stothert, was devoting a disproportionate amount of his time to the Bath-based engineering firm of Stothert & Pitt, of which he was the managing partner. Unfortunately, Avonside's financial position became even worse over the next three years, and in July 1881 a liquidation order was issued against the company, before it was put up for sale in March 1882. Avonside's

The Avonside Engine Company's 1916–17 season football team.

machinery, patterns and spares were subsequently acquired by Edwin Walker, recently a partner in the defunct locomotive builders Fox Walker, who also leased part of the site from its new owner John Mardon.

In order to obtain maximum benefit from the old company, Walker traded as the Avonside Engine Company but in the 1880s was forced to rely upon general engineering work to keep his business afloat as during that decade the firm only manufactured two locomotives.

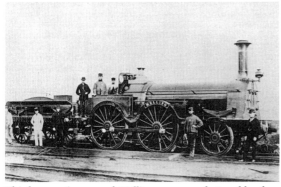

This locomotive named *Melling* was manufactured by the newly constituted Avonside Engineering Company in 1865 for the Great Western Railway.

Nevertheless, before the end of the 19th century the market for small saddle tank engines suitable for industrial and narrow gauge railways really started to expand both at home and abroad, and soon over half of Avonside's production was being exported.

Consequently, the company outgrew its St Philip's premises, and when Ronald Murray joined Walker in partnership in 1904 he brought with him enough capital to enable Avonside to relocate to a new factory on a four-acre site alongside the railway station in Fishponds. Here the firm had provision for a machine shop, a smithy, a boiler shop, a pattern shop, an erecting shop and a paint shop, the whole complex employing some 300 men when the order books were full.

The following year Edwin Walker retired, after which his son, Edwin Webster Walker, took over as senior partner until his premature death in 1909. After this the Avonside Engine Company became a private limited company under the control of Ronald Murray and Vivian Gordon, a well-known hotelier. During World War One Avonside continued with locomotive production, and during the 1920s trade remained buoyant as domestic operators undertook large replacement programmes and export markets continued to generate substantial orders.

However, by the 1930s sales both at home and overseas collapsed, and with the whole British locomotive industry in a state of great distress it was not surprising that many firms went to the wall. Avonside was one victim, and after going into liquidation in November 1934 the Fishponds works finally closed early the following year, after which the company's goodwill, drawings, patterns and spares were acquired by the Hunslett Engine Company of Leeds.

Peckett & Sons

The other famous and long lived Bristol locomotive manufacturer was Fox, Walker and Company, probably better known locally as Pecketts, an undertaking that, although not one of the early pioneers of the railway industry, nevertheless, was still in business some 20 years after Avonside had failed. It owed its existence not to the requirements of a rapidly expanding national railway system, but rather to the increasing demand created during the 1860s for robust shunting engines and small industrial locomotives that could be cheaply built to standard designs.

The firm's founder was one Francis William Fox Walker, a member of a Quaker banking family from Kingsbridge in Devon who, after training as a railway engineer, had moved to Bristol where, in 1864, he entered into partnership with Edwin Walker, another engineer with a Quaker background. Fox, Walker & Company established their new Atlas works on a site in Deep Pit Road, St George, conveniently situated adjacent to the short Midland Railway branch line, which ran from Kingswood Junction up to Speedwell colliery.

During the first four years of trading the new firm produced a large number of small tank engines for use in civil engineering projects and on large industrial sites, some 40 percent of which were sent overseas. The early 1870s saw Fox Walker expand into the field of narrow gauge railways, but although between 1864 and 1878 the company's 200 or so workers had pro-

A saddle tank locomotive named *Bristol*, manufactured by Fox, Walker & Co. at their Atlas works in Deep Pit Road, St George.

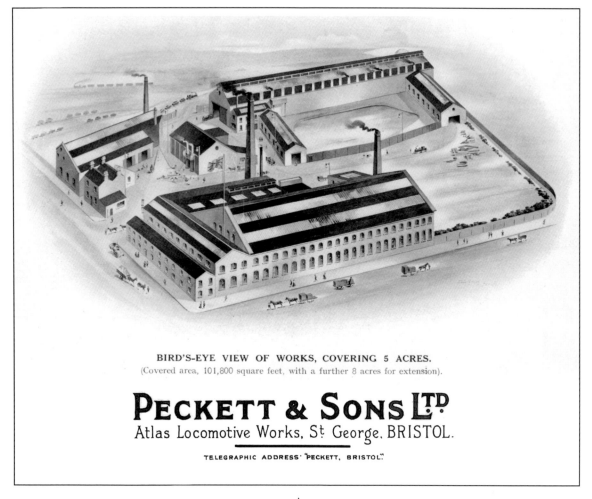

BIRD'S-EYE VIEW OF WORKS, COVERING 5 ACRES.
(Covered area, 101,800 square feet, with a further 8 acres for extension).

PECKETT & SONS L™

Atlas Locomotive Works, S! George. BRISTOL.

TELEGRAPHIC ADDRESS· 'PECKETT, BRISTOL."

duced some 424 locomotives, further attempts at diversification failed. Consequently, with mounting losses the partnership was dissolved in December 1878.

A saviour, however, was at hand, and in 1881 the Atlas Works was taken over by a Birmingham engineer named Thomas Peckett, who was soon joined by his sons, George, John, Thomas II and Richard. Peckett & Sons quickly settled down to building industrial locomotives to a standard design in much the same way as the previous proprietors, and so successful were they that during the first half of the 20th century the company's name was almost synonymous with industrial saddle tank engines. These the company considered were 'eminently suitable for branch lines, mineral lines, steel and iron works, gas works, tinplate works, collieries and all kinds of contractors work.'

Although Thomas Peckett died in 1890, under George's leadership, the firm continued to expand, and in order to keep up with demand a new machine shop was built and the boiler shop modernised. As a result, in 1905, by which time the works covered over a third of their 13-acre site, Pecketts were able to boast that 'The engines are manufactured by skilled workmen in buildings especially designed and erected to obtain the maximum amount of light and convenience for the proper execution of the work.' In addition, their policy of standardisation and specialisation helped to maintain the company's firm financial base, and although drastic cuts in employee numbers had to be made during the economic storms of the 1930s Pecketts continued to manufacture their famous little tank engines until well after World War Two.

However, during the early 1950s, by which time the company was being run by George Peckett's sons, Frank, Wilfred and Roy, the days of the

The erecting and finishing shop at Peckett & Sons' Atlas Locomotive Works, St George.

steam locomotive were numbered as industrial users increasingly switched over to more cost-effective Diesel traction. In spite of the obvious writing on the wall, the firm still remained reluctant to embrace the new technology, and it was only after Frank Peckett's retirement in 1954 that a belated attempt was made to build diesel locomotives, of which only five were ever completed.

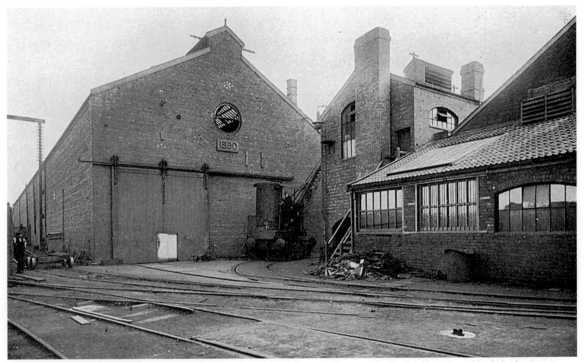

A view into the yard of Peckett & Sons' Atlas Locomotive Works at St George. The Boiler Shop is on the left, the Brass Foundry in the centre and the Coppersmith's Shop on the right.

In the Machine Shop of Peckett & Sons' Atlas Locomotive Works at St George looking westwards.

The end was now in sight for the company, and after the last steam locomotive left the Atlas Works in June 1958 Peckett & Sons passed into history.

Sad though the demise of Avonside and Pecketts was, both companies had done much to demonstrate Bristol's engineering skill at home and abroad, and today the odd survivors of the 6,200 or so engines they produced should serve to remind people of when the city really was a centre of international importance in locomotive engineering.

Carts, Wagons and Carriages

The process of transforming the roads around Bristol from little more than dirt tracks into modern multi-lane highways really began in 1727 with the turnpiking of some 12 of the most important roads leading out of the city into its hinterland. Locally the work of gating, collecting the tolls and carrying out the necessary repairs and improvements fell to the Bristol Turnpike Trust which, by the 1820s, was the largest in the country, controlling some 180 miles of roads. With an improvement in the condition of the

local roads came an increased demand for horse-drawn carts, wagons and carriages of all kinds, something which a growing number of local firms sought to satisfy.

Perry & Company's old Carriage Works in Stokes Croft. It is hoped to restore and convert this Grade II listed building, designed in 1862 by Edward Godwin, into a regional and national flagship centre for black culture.

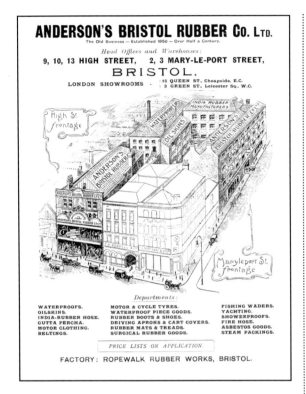

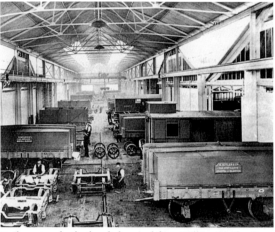

Railway trucks for local chemical firm William Butler & Co. under construction at the Bristol Wagon & Carriage Works at Lawrence Hill, *c.*1906.

Notable among these were John Fuller & Company of St George's Road, founded way back in 1777, Rogers & Company of College Place and Perry & Company of Stokes Croft, established in 1804, a firm which in 1862 had a new two-acre works built for them to the designs of local architect Edward Godwin. This was the building taken over in 1912 by Anderson's Bristol Rubber Company, which had moved from its previous High Street/Mary Le Port Street and Ropewalk premises and today the Grade II listed part of the original complex awaits restoration and conversion into an arts centre.

Bristol Wagon & Carriage Works Company

In the same way as the early 19th century had seen an upturn in demand for road vehicles, the arrival of the railways saw at least three Bristol-based undertakings involve themselves in the construction of rolling stock, in particular wagons destined for private undertakings such as collieries. As the skills required for such work were very similar to those needed for building road vehicles, local firms were soon engaged in this type of work. Although both the Bristol & South Wales Railway Wagon Company and the Western Wagon Company had been established back in 1860 it was the Bristol Wagon & Carriage Works Company that went on to become the largest and most important.

Its origins can be traced back to the 1840s

when Fowler & Fry set up business in Portwall Lane, John Fry, one of the partners, being the inventor of a steam plough. Within 20 years the concern was trading as Messrs Albert & Theodore Fry, iron founders, wheelwrights, agricultural implement and machine makers, and in order for them to raise sufficient capital to expand into the production of railway wagons, trucks and carriages, in 1866 they set up the Bristol Wagon Works Company.

The Fry brothers chose Lawrence Hill to set up their new works, and, with Albert Fry as managing director, by 1883 the Bristol Wagon Works Company Ltd site covered an area of some 12

BRISTOL WAGON WORKS COMPANY, LIMITED.
RAILWAY CARRIAGE,
AND
WAGON BUILDERS,
AGRICULTURAL IMPLEMENT MAKERS.

OFFICES AND WORKS:—LAWRENCE HILL.
IMPLEMENT WAREHOUSE & SHOWROOMS:—
VICTORIA STREET, near the Railway Station.

A view inside the Bristol Wagon & Carriage Works at Lawrence Hill showing railway carriages under construction.

acres. Here were employed some 900 people who still produced agricultural vehicles and machinery alongside the rolling stock, and by the end of the 19th century the firm was operating very successfully, with much of its output going for export. During the early years of the 20th century it was already in the business of supplying a range of gas and petrol engines, as well as manufacturing motor car bodies, an activity also undertaken by rivals John Fuller & Company. The Bristol Wagon & Carriage Works Company Ltd, as it was later known, continued as an independently run concern until 1920, when it was taken over by the Leeds Forge Company. In 1923 they in turn amalgamated with Cammell Laird, an organisation which saw fit to close down the Bristol operation.

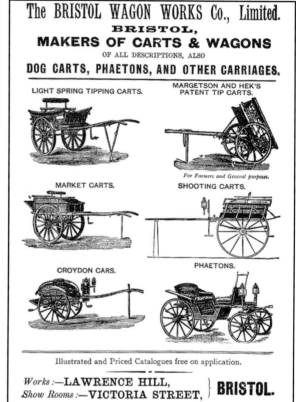

OWEN, BRAZIL & CO.,
ENGINEERS,
Vulcan Iron Works,
AVONSIDE,
❖ BRISTOL. ❖

CONTRACTORS FOR

ALL KINDS OF MACHINERY,
HYDRAULIC, STEAM & HAND POWER

CRANES, LIFTS & HOISTS,

Centrifugal, Direct-Acting and other PUMPS.

Hydraulic Machine Tools and Pressing Machinery,

BREWERY PLANT,

STEAM ENGINES, GENERAL MILL-GEARING,

AND ALL KINDS OF

METAL STAMPING WORK.

Special Staff of Workmen kept for Repairs and Breakdowns.

The Brazil Straker Company

Following on from the railway revolution of the mid-19th century came the start of a similar upheaval in road transport as horse power gave way to steam power and the internal combustion engine at the dawn of the 20th century. Although the original Bristol Motor Company, founded towards the end of the 1890s, produced a 'Bristol' motor car between 1901 and 1909, one local firm went on to develop both steam and petrol-driven vehicles.

The company's entry into this field was due mainly to the enthusiasm of an Irishman named Joseph Peter Brazil, who had served his apprenticeship with the Gloucester Wagon Company. After moving to Bristol in 1893 the young Brazil entered into partnership with a Mr Owen at the Vulcan Iron Works in Chapel Street, St Philips

Marsh. Here, trading as Owen, Brazil & Co, they manufactured such things as Bonzac cigarette processing machinery for W.D. & H.O. Wills, parts for Spencer Moulton hydraulic railway buffers and Djinn marine engines, as well as making a range of castings and forgings to order.

Additional premises in nearby Grafton Street and Albert Road were soon acquired, and in 1897 a local engineer named Holborow joined the partnership, which was then renamed Owen, Brazil & Holborow. Two years later the firm became a limited company. One of their customers was the Straker Steam Vehicle Company of London, the proprietors of which were Sidney Starker and Mr I.L.R. Squire, who looked after the sales and servicing side of the company. Owen, Brazil & Holborow began by casting and machining steam omnibus parts for them, but so close did their collaboration become that complete chassis were soon being built at the Vulcan Iron Works. Finally, the relationship was formalised in 1901 when Owen retired and Straker took his place as a partner.

However, it soon became obvious that the future lay with the internal combustion engine, and so, with this in mind, Brazil, Straker and Squire resolved to design and build a double-decker motor omnibus to be powered by the German Bussing engine. As before, it was

Part of the workforce pose for the camera outside the Brazil Straker Company's Fishponds Motor Works at Lodge Causeway, *c.*1910.

arranged that the chassis part was to be made in Bristol and the bodies fitted in London. The first of these vehicles began operating in the capital in March 1906, and by July 1907 over 300 Straker-Squire buses had entered service. In order to increase their manufacturing capacity, a new London depot was established at Blackfriars where it traded as Sidney Straker & Squire, while in Bristol a four-acre site in Lodge Causeway, Fishponds, was purchased, on which an entirely new factory was laid out in 1907.

A 1906 24 hp Straker-Squire Bussing motor omnibus being operated by the London General Omnibus Company.

During the same year Holborow finally retired, allowing the Bristol firm to be changed from Brazil, Holborow & Straker to the Brazil Straker Company. As Peter Brazil was also a shareholder and supplier to W.D. & H.O. Wills, the production of the Bonzac cigarette processing machines was also transferred from the Vulcan Works to Lodge Causeway, where some 300 men were soon being employed. The working conditions there were good as the works was not only well planned and airy but had also been designed to accommodate many self-contained electrically-powered machines. These were a great deal safer to operate than those relying on the steam-driven overhead belting system, which was still in use in many factories.

During 1907 around 70 bus engines a month were being manufactured at Fishponds, and during that year the Brazil Straker Company were fortunate enough to acquire the services of an up and coming young engineer named Roy Fedden. He quickly set about designing a new motor car, which he called the Shamrock, as a tribute to his new Irish employer. This was a great success and developed into the 15hp Straker-Squire with a

Straker-Squire racing cars photographed outside the Fishponds Motor Works in 1914.

price tag of £315, which went on to sell about 150 during the 1908–09 season.

In the years that followed some 1,300 cars were produced, due in part to the success at Brooklands in the Scottish, Irish and 2,000 mile trials and in the Tourist Trophy races in the Isle of Man, and before long the factory was turning out about 12 a week. The bus business also flourished and by the end of 1909 around 1,000 had been supplied to London alone. Prior to 1914 Straker-Squire buses were also being operated by transport undertakings in places as diverse as Torquay, Bath, Worthing, Brighton, Preston and Cambridge, while during World War One the Brazil Straker Company undertook the manufacture of over 750,000 shells for the War Office, as well as building staff cars and heavy lorries for military use.

The Cosmos Engineering Company

At the outbreak of World War One the Brazil Straker Company of Fishponds obtained a contract to overhaul American Curtiss OX-5 aero engines, but their Chief Engineer Roy Fedden became so successful in improving these that the firm were rewarded with the rare honour of a contract to manufacture Rolls-Royce Hawk and

Falcon engines. Under Fedden's control, no less than 2,500 of these were built at Fishponds, but as part of the agreement Brazil Straker were not permitted to design any liquid cooled engine of their

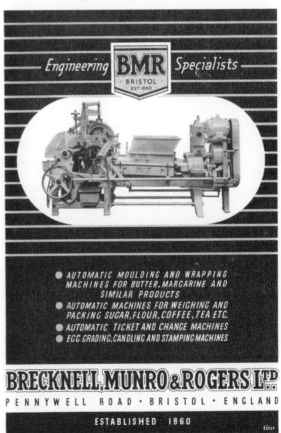

own until seven years after they had ceased building Rolls-Royce engines.

The Fishponds works also produced a number of French designed Renault air-cooled engines, and, consequently, in 1917 this led the Air Ministry to ask the Brazil Straker Company to design an aero engine weighing less than 600lbs. The result was the 300hp 'Mercury', which was first tested in 1918, the same year in which Fedden unveiled his second engine, the 450hp 'Jupiter'. Unfortunately, these attracted the attention of a newly formed Anglo-American financial named Cosmos, the primary interests of which were shipping and coal and, as a result, in 1918 they took over the Brazil Straker Company, after which time the Fishponds works became known as the Cosmos Engineering Company.

Peter Brazil then joined the Cosmos Board of Directors, and an imaginative plan was conceived whereby Fishponds would be developed as a tool room and experimental centre at the heart of a group of Cosmos factories established in various parts of the country. This, however, came to nothing as one of Cosmos's directors objected on religious grounds to the company's involvement with cigarette production machinery, leading to Peter Brazil departing to join local engineering concern Brecknell, Munro & Rogers, who were delighted to acquire his Bonzac manufacturing licence.

At that time Brecknell, Munro & Rogers was already a well-established concern, having been founded as a small brass foundry and engineer's shop in Lawrence Hill in 1858, where it had been principally engaged in manufacturing steam fittings. The founder's son, Henry, further expanded the business, which went on to specialise in the installation and maintenance of gas engines. By the late 19th century the undertaking could boast one of the largest brass and aluminium foundries in the West of England, and in 1896 Mr E.M. Munro joined as a partner, as did Mr H.I. Rogers two years later.

Rather unwisely, Cosmos also sold off the Djinn marine engine side of the business to a shipbuilding firm, while the entire car manufacturing and design operation was passed on to Straker-Squire Ltd of Edmonton, London. However, this was a relatively short lived undertaking as it ceased trading in 1926, not long after Sidney Straker had been killed in a hunting accident. With these valuable revenue-generating assets gone, it proved impossible for Cosmos to properly finance its aero engine development work, and matters finally came to a head in 1919 when a large export consignment of household goods destined for White Russia was seized by the Blosheviks.

This forced Cosmos into liquidation, and in March 1920 the Air Ministry succeeded in persuading the directors of the Bristol Aeroplane Company to acquire its aero engine assets. Finally, in 1923 Cosmos Engineering's old Lodge Causeway site was taken over by Parnall & Sons Ltd, the well-known shop fitting company which, in 1934, extended their premises by absorbing the adjoining Avonside locomotive works.

Douglas Motors Ltd

Another early entrant into the field of vehicle construction was the Douglas Engineering Co, whose motorcycles were at one time held in great regard in places as far apart as Australia and New Zealand, Japan, Austria, South Africa and Spain. Their extensive factory was located in Kingswood, and many of the local people employed there spent the whole of their working lives with the company.

Towards the end of the 19th century, William, Edward and Arthur Douglas, three brothers from a family that originally hailed from Greenock in Scotland, settled in Bristol. Here William took up employment as a journeyman mechanic, his job being to repair the sewing machines used in the Kingswood boot and shoe factories. Although Arthur soon left to try his luck in Australia, the two remaining brothers decided to go into busi-

ness together, and in 1882 William rented a small house and workshop where they were able to set up a blacksmith's shop. Within a few years the business had expanded to such an extent that Douglas & Company were forced to relocate to new premises in the vicinity of today's Kingswood Council Depot where they were able to establish a fully fledged iron foundry.

Here, for the next 20 years, the Douglas's undertook the manufacture of such diverse items as lasts for the boot and shoe industry, lampposts, drain gratings and manhole covers, many of which still survive in the Bristol area. They also began to produce castings for Joseph Barter, a Bedminster engineer, whose Light Motors Ltd went on to develop a horizontal twin-cylinder engine called the Fairy, capable of being fitted on to a standard cycle frame.

Although Barter's firm soon went into liquidation, it was taken over by Douglas, who set up their own motorcycle department, which Joe Bater was employed to run. In 1907 they launched their first motorcycle, and, although only about

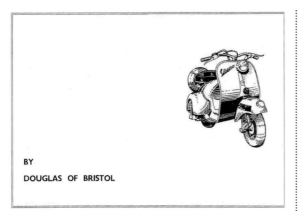

BY
DOUGLAS OF BRISTOL

An aerial view of Douglas Motors Ltd's extensive works at Kingswood, with Hanham Road in the foreground and Forest Road in the background.

The Frame Building Department at Douglas's Kingswood Factory.

Harry Lorraine about to set off on a 6,000-mile ride around the United Kingdom in 1926. His mount is a Douglas E.W. motorcycle.

10 a week were built during the next seven years, competition success soon established their reputation as a manufacturer of high performance bikes. This led, in 1914, to Douglas Engineering being offered a War Office contract to produce some 300 machines a week for Army dispatch riders, and a new factory, which at its peak employed some 3,000 people, was built for this purpose in Hanham Road.

'Second to None' was the Douglas motto, and this was certainly true during 1923 when the company's bikes not only won the Senior and Sidecar TT races in the Isle of Man but also held about 150 British and World Speed Records! However, 'Dougie's' were expensive and, with a price tag of £80 for a 500cc machine, were well beyond the reach of all but the well heeled. Unfortunately, the new EW model introduced in 1925 was initially of such poor quality that heavy warranty claims quickly resulted, while problems of unpaid tax amounting to between £5 and £10 million pounds and a disastrous fire in 1926 all conspired against the company. Nevertheless, Douglas fought back, and in 1928 the firm entered into another boom period with the arrival in Britain of the new sport of speedway racing, something for which Douglas motorcycles, with their low centre of gravity, were well suited. Consequently, in 1929 some 1,300 speedway bikes were produced by the firm.

DOUGLAS ANNUAL SPORTS & CARNIVAL
KINGSWOOD GROUND
July 2nd, 3rd, & 5th.
CHAMPIONSHIPS   ::   CYCLING   ::   RUNNING

Some of the action from Douglas's 1926 sports & carnival.

Sadly, the company was to enjoy only a short-lived revival, and although Douglas Motors Ltd managed to struggle through the early 1930s by augmenting its motorcycle production with the manufacture of such things as lightweight aircraft engines and industrial trucks, the financial problems soon became insurmountable. Consequently, in mid-1935 the Douglas family's connection with the firm was finally severed when their proud old undertaking passed into the hands of the Bristol Aeroplane Company. This, coupled with the death of his two sons, had a profound effect upon the founder, and in April 1937 William Douglas passed away at the age of 78.

The business then began trading under the name of Aero Engines Ltd, as it had been anticipated that a contract to build Hispano Suiza aircraft engines under licence was about to be awarded. This, however, did not materialise, and so the firm continued with the limited manufacture of motorcycles, assembled mostly from spare parts already in stock. Consequently, by the outbreak of World War Two the company was virtually at a standstill, and, as no contract was awarded for military motorcycles, during the con-

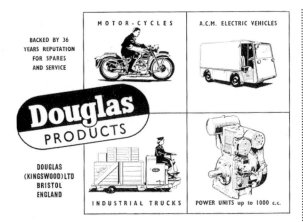

flict the Kingswood factory was mainly engaged in work for the Ministry of Aircraft Production and the manufacture of industrial trucks.

A return to peace saw motorcycle production resumed with the 350cc Mk I, and although they got off to a good start serious financial problems soon arose, which resulted in the appointment of an Official Receiver and the reforming of the company as Douglas (Kingswood) Ltd. Although they continued to build motorcycles, the firm were soon forced to look to other products, and in 1950 they entered into an agreement to produce Vespa motor scooters for the Italian company Piaggio.

Likewise, new regulations, which banned vehicles with internal combustion engines from operating in food storage areas, also gave the Douglas's the opportunity to develop a range of electric delivery vans. Even this was not enough to save the company, and following a further financial crisis in 1956 it was acquired by the Westinghouse Brake & Signal Company. During the following year production of the last Douglas motorcycle, the famous 'Dragonfly', finally came to an end, although Vespas continued to be made until 1964, by which time a total of 126,000 had been built at Kingswood.

The Douglas Company itself was taken over in 1970 by the Bendix Corporation of America and, trading under the name of Bendix Ltd, the factory was turned over to the manufacture of braking systems for the automobile industry. However, Douglas (Sales & Service) Ltd, which imported small capacity Gilera motorcycles and Vespa scooters direct from Piaggio, lived on, relocated to the Fishponds Trading Estate, and survived until being acquired by Vespa (UK) Ltd, a Heron

Part of the old Douglas factory in 2005. This photograph shows the Douglas Road entrance.

In 2005 Douglas Motors Ltd's old office block was still surviving in Hanham Road.

Corporation Company, which, during June 1982, transferred the operation to Crawley in Sussex.

Bristol Commercial Vehicles

Although both Starker-Squire and Douglas did much to put Bristol on the map as a vehicle-building city, two other companies, one large and one small, have also ensured that Bristol's reputation as a manufacturing centre for quality motor vehicles has continued until the present day. Confusingly, over the years both have used the title 'Bristol', this being made possible by that fact that over the years it has proved impossible to register this as a trademark for an individual concern.

Back in 1908 the Bristol Tramways & Carriage Company, the undertaking responsible for operating the city's tramcar network, decided to

inally employed, the company soon decided to manufacture its own vehicles. To begin with the engines and chassis were produced at the company's Filton works erected specially in 1908 and the bodies at the Brislington tram depot, but in 1913 a new Motor Constructional Works was opened on Kensington Hill, just a short distance up the hill from the tram depot, in premises built in 1902 for Charles Bartlett & Company, scale makers.

After a break in production caused by World War One, during the 1920s the company began to make its vehicles available to operators in such diverse places as Cornwall, Sunderland, Aberdare and Manchester, while the first double-deckers to be manufactured went to Hull. During 1935 the Bristol Tramways & Carriage Company became a part of the Thomas Tilling Group of operators and soon the group began to standardise around the Bristol chassis, which were normally bodied by the Eastern Coach Works at Lowestoft, another member of the Tilling Group. This ensured that the Brislington works received a steady flow of orders, which was supplemented by manufacturing buses for a number of operators outside the Tilling Group.

expand its routes by the introduction of motor buses. However, as Bristol's hills proved too much of a challenge for the Thornycroft and Fiats orig-

A Bristol two-ton, single decker bus undergoing a clinometer test at Brislington, *c*.1925.

"*Bristol*"

PASSENGER VEHICLES

ADD LUSTRE TO

A FAMOUS NAME

MANUFACTURED AND OPERATED BY
THE BRISTOL TRAMWAYS & CARRIAGE CO. LTD.

Bristol Commercial Vehicles Limited
Bath Road,
Brislington,
Bristol 4.
Telephone Bristol 77613

BRISTOL

Perhaps the best known buses produced during the 1930s were the 'B Type' single-decker, of which some 778 were made between 1929 and 1934, and the 'K Type' double-deckers and 'L Type' single-deckers, which were introduced in 1937, some 7,500 of these eventually being made. Both were fitted with Gardner diesel engines and these rugged vehicles soon became famous for their reliability and economy. With so much work on the books, additional space was required and in 1935 the nearby Chatsworth Road works was acquired and laid out as a chassis assembly section.

World War Two caused a further break in bus manufacturing, and for the second time in a quarter of a century the Brislington factory went over to aeronautical work. However, during the conflict the country's bus fleet suffered badly, and in 1944 the company was selected as one of only three UK manufacturers to be permitted to restart double-decker production. In 1946 an export drive was started, and as a result Bristol-built buses were sent as far afield as India, South Africa and New Zealand. National-

isation came the following year and the restricting clauses of the 1947 Transport Act subsequently prevented the company from supplying bus chassis to any organisation otrher than the Thomas Tilling Group or the Scottish Omnibus Group.

In September 1948 the Tilling Group sold all their interests in road transport to the British Transport Commission, and as the number of state-owned operators increased so did the output of the Brislington works. In addition to bus chassis, the company also began manufacturing a heavy goods vehicle chassis to its own design for publicly owned British Road Services, and the HG, as it was known, remained in production from 1952 until 1955.

Bristol Commercial Vehicles prototype eight-wheeler lorry, photographed in 1952.

Chassis manufacture at Bristol Commercial Vehicles' Chatsworth Road site.

Bristol Commercial Vehicles' Kensington Hill premises. The main Bath Road is in the background, while the old Brislington Tram Depot can be seen in the top right hand corner.

The sign that once graced the entrance to Bristol Commercial Vehicles' Kensington Hill site.

Nevertheless, important bus development work also continued, and 1954 saw the introduction of the famous 'Lodekka', a revolutionary low decked double-decker, which had its engine fitted under the floor. The following year the manufacturing arm of the Bristol Tramways & Carriage Company effectively became a separate company when it was renamed Bristol Commercial Vehicles Ltd, and in 1962 they introduced the 'Bristol RE', a 36-feet long rear-engined bus designed to operate on fairly busy routes.

At last, in 1965, as a result of a government share swap with British Leyland Motor Corpor-ation, Bristol Commercial Vehicles were no longer restricted to selling to state-owned operators, and the following year they introduced the famous 'VR', a rear engined double-decker, which was to be the last pure Bristol design manufactured by Bristol Commercial Vehicles. This became the standard double-decker for the National Bus Company until the introduction of the Leyland 'Olympian' in 1981, which ironically had been designed and initially built at the Brislington works. The last Bristol 'VR' came off the Brislington production line in August 1981, just at a time when there was a sharp downturn in the bus market, and after they had produced only 1,000 'Olympian' chassis, Leyland, by then in sole

Workers from Bristol Commercial Vehicles outside the Council House in 1983, taking part in a demonstration against the closure of the company.

charge of the Bristol factory, ordered that manufacturing should be transferred to their plant at Workington in Cumbria. This spelt the end for Bristol Commercial Vehicles, and in August 1983 the factory closed its gates for the last time with the loss of 530 jobs. Although the old Brislington tram depot still survives, the whole of Bristol Commercial Vehicles Kensington Hill site was demolished to make way for Tramway Road, which leads to a mini trading estate containing a 'Great Mills' outlet and a 'Focus' DIY store, while the Chatsworth Road chassis works has been replaced by a new building housing Bryan Brothers 'Citroen' dealership.

Bristol Cars Ltd

In spite of the fact that buses and lorries are no longer produced in Bristol, the city's name is still proudly carried by a small number of motor vehicles. However, these high-powered sports cars could hardly be more different to the Bristol-built buses, which over the years established a worldwide reputation for longevity and reliability. The story of Bristol Cars begins at the end of World War Two

when the Bristol Aeroplane Company at Filton, faced with a huge surplus of skilled labour and a need to diversify into alternative products, decided to enter the quality car market. To this end the rights were acquired as war reparations for the manufacture of pre-war BMW engines and cars.

A car division was quickly established, and in 1947 the two-litre 'Type 400' was launched, these superbly designed vehicles made from top quality materials regardless of cost soon establishing an enviable reputation for Bristol cars. The 'Type 401' followed in 1948, and this numerical sequence continued so that by 1955 the '405' was the model then in production. In 1956 the Bristol Car Division became a separate subsidiary of the

A cutaway drawing of the Bristol Type 401. This two-litre car was produced between 1948 and 1953.

Outside a hanger at the Filton works a Bristol Type 404 car, manufactured between 1953 and 1955, poses in front of a Type Bristol 405, in production from 1954 until 1958.

Bristol Aeroplane Company, and in 1960 George White, the grandson of the founder of the BAC, together with Anthony Cook, a former Grand Prix racing driver, acquired the company, which was then retitled Bristol Cars Ltd. The following year they introduced the 'Type 407' fitted with an American Chrysler 5130cc V8 engine, the first Bristol car to employ a power plant not designed and built at Filton.

In 1966 the status of the company was changed from that of a limited company to that of a firm in private partnership. This, however, was a relatively short lived arrangement, for in 1973, when Sir George White as he was then known, finally retired, Cook became the sole proprietor and Managing Director, at which time he changed the company status back to that of a limited company. By 1975 Bristol Cars had finally broken into the potentially lucrative American market after switching production to a left hand drive version of the 'Type 12' convertible saloon, and in 1980 Bristol began naming their cars after famous Filton built aircrafts, the first to appear being the 'Beaufighter', followed in 1982 by the 'Brigand'.

One of their most recent offerings has been the gull wing two-seater 'Bristol Fighter' with a price tag of more than £229,000 but with a top speed 210mph, making it the world's second fastest production car. Although only about 20 of these hand-built cars are manufactured each year, at its launch in May 2003 Managing Director Tony

Cook stated that 'Bristol Cars is the only luxury car manufacturer that remains in private British hands. This ensures us absolute independence of thought and action that is essential to our purpose. Fighter is one of the very few cars ever designed where aerodynamic efficiency has been placed ahead of all other considerations. Innovation in design features are shared with aircraft, high-speed missiles and even submarines.'

The British & Colonial Aeroplane Company

The establishment of a world famous aircraft industry in Bristol, which for many years was by far the area's largest employer, was really due to the entrepreneurial skills of one man universally remembered today as Sir George White, Bart. LLD, JP. Born in Bristol in 1854, the young George left school at the age of 14 and after becoming articled to a solicitor was soon handling most of his employers bankruptcy business, much of it railway related. This work led to a lifelong interest in transportation systems, and, after some teething troubles had been experienced in the establishment of a tramway network in his home city, in 1875 George White, still only 21 years of age, was appointed Secretary of the Bristol Tramways Company.

Sir George was interested in all forms of transport and since 1904 had been carefully observing the progress being made in aviation. Consequently, at a Bristol Tramways & Carriage

The Bristol Boxkite assembly line at Filton, *c.*1910.

Company shareholders' meeting held on 16 February 1910 he announced his intention of opening an aircraft factory, and just three days later he launched the British & Colonial Aeroplane Company Ltd with a capital of £25,000. In addition, three other companies, the Bristol Aeroplane Company Ltd, the Bristol Aviation Company Ltd and the British & Colonial Aviation Company Ltd, each with a nominal capital of £100, were also formed.

Back in the 1880s George White had moved to Fairlawn House in Filton, and although he moved away in 1907 he still owned the property and an adjoining two acres of land, upon which in the following year he built, for the Bristol Tramways & Carriage Company, a chassis manufacturing works and a garage for taxicab maintenance, which also acted as a depot for the buses running out to Thornbury. It was these two sheds that were to be used as a fledgling aircraft factory, the chief engineer of which was to be the young George Challenger, who was already employed as Foreman at the Bristol Tramways & Carriage Company's bus works.

Aeroplane Flights on the Downs.
"BRISTOL" BIPLANES
BUILT IN BRISTOL BY BRISTOL MEN.
OFFICIAL STATEMENT.

REQUEST TO THE PUBLIC.

An aeroplane display, reasonable weather provided, will be given on the Downs to-morrow afternoon by the flyers of the British and Colonial Aeroplane Company.

We have received the following letter containing this interesting intimation :—

(To the Editor of " Evening Times and Echo.")

Sir,—Under the auspices of the Bristol and West of England Aero Club, the directors of the British and Colonial Aeroplane Company are proposing to afford their fellow citizens the opportunity of witnessing some demonstrations of aviation, which will take place on Durdham Downs as the only public space available and suitable for the purpose.

Weather circumstances, including the whole gamut of wind, rain, fog, etc., will necessarily control the operations and make it impossible to announce a more definite programme ; but, subject to these conditions being favourable, the demonstrations will take place each day for the next few days, excluding, of course, Sunday.

As these flying exhibitions are being provided quite gratuitously and no space will be enclosed, we rely with full confidence on the goodwill and sportsmanlike behaviour of the spectators to keep clear of two spaces only, namely :—

(1) The entire plateau near the Sea Walls (where the Territorials usually parade and drill), and

(2) The space, between the Stoke and Westbury Roads, inside the white posts.

so that the aviators may have unimpeded freedom to manœuvre, ascend or alight on any of those areas.

It is also desirable that the roadways of the Downs should be kept clear for the free passage of motors in case of emergency.

Representatives of the football clubs have kindly undertaken that there shall be no goal-posts standing except during the actual time of play on Saturday afternoon.

We desire publicly to acknowledge the generous assistance accorded by the Downs Committee, on whose behalf the Lord Mayor has courteously granted the necessary facilities for the provisions of the temporary hangars and otherwise.

We feel sure that the spectators will be equally willing to do everything in their power individually, by the exercise of patience, restraint and good order, to ensure the success of this novel entertainment for Bristolians.

Yours faithfully,

GEORGE WHITE,
Chairman, Aeroplane Company.

HERBERT ASHMAN,
Vice-President, Aero Club.

Bristol, 11th November, 1910.

In November 1910 the French pilot Maurice Tetard gave the first public demonstration of an aircraft produced by the British & Colonial Aeroplane Company. Two 'Bristol Biplanes' were taken to Durdham Down in Bristol and were flown from there for the benefit of local people.

Bristol Fighters under construction in the assembly hall at Filton during 1918.

To ensure that production started as quickly as possible, the British & Colonial Aeroplane Company obtained a manufacturing licence from Société Zodiac in France, but after the Bristol 'Zodiac' aircraft proved unable to fly the project was abandoned. Instead the firm pinned their hopes on a new machine designed by George Challenger, and this was much more successful, the Bristol 'Boxkite', as it was unofficially called, making its first flight on Salisbury Plain on 30 July 1910.

The new machine went into production in 1911 and by the end of 1912 over 80 had been manufactured. In order to facilitate this, what Sir George White described as the largest aircraft factory in the world had been established at Filton. Here, land to the north of the two original sheds had also been acquired to lay out an airfield, additional buildings erected and an office opened in Filton House. During the next couple of years the company went on to develop several types of biplane, culminating in the small and fast single-seater Bristol 'Scout', the prototype of which appeared in February 1914. Following the outbreak of war in August of that year the Filton complex was rapidly expanded, and by the time

the Armistice was finally signed in November 1918 the British & Colonial Aeroplane Company had more that 3,000 employees, who between them were building some 2,000 military aeroplanes a year.

Of all the aircraft manufactured by the company during World War One, by far the most famous was the Bristol 'Fighter', of which about 3,500 were produced between 1916 and 1927. In order to accommodate the large orders that were placed during the conflict the Tramways Company's motor works at Brislington was also pressed into service, and by the end of 1916 some 370 'Scouts' had been built there. This, however, was only the start, and by the time production ceased there in September 1919 a total of 1,045 'Bristol Fighters' had been assembled.

George Parnall & Company

World War One also saw another Bristol firm enter into the field of aircraft manufacture for the first time as a result of gaining contracts from the Admiralty, one of these being Parnall & Sons, a firm whose origins can be traced back to 1820 when William Parnall established a weights and measures manufacturing business in Narrow

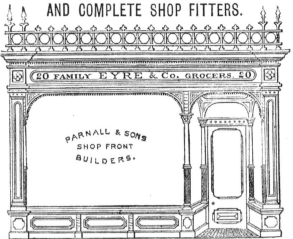
Wine Street, Bristol. It became a limited company in 1889 under the title of Parnall & Sons Ltd, and during the following decade expanded, gaining a high reputation for the quality of its products as well as for the shop fitting work it was then undertaking. This drew the company to the attention of W & T Avery, the Birmingham weights and measures manufacturer, which, in

1898, acquired a controlling interest in Parnall & Sons Ltd.

In 1923 Parnall & Sons Ltd moved to a site in Lodge Causeway, Fishponds, previously occupied by Cosmos Engineering, and in 1931 Tansad, a firm manufacturing office furniture, joined the Parnall operation. During World War Two a variety of wooden aircraft components were manufactured by Parnall & Sons Ltd, but after hostilities had ceased they switched back to their traditional high-quality shop fitting work. However, after over three decades of relative prosperity, in 1979 the company was taken over by GEC, who in turn sold it on to C.H. Holdings, a London-based conglomerate. Unfortunately, while in their possession the Fishponds factory suffered several serious fires, and in May 1991 Parnall & Sons Ltd went into receivership with closure following shortly after. Since then the existing buildings have been gradually demolished so that by 2005 little is left to remind local people of the once

A look inside Parnalls Lodge Causeway works showing the manufacture of shopfittings.

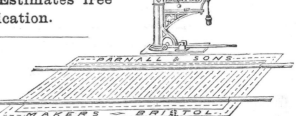
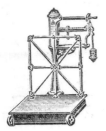

flourishing concern, which for so many years was an important Fishponds landmark.

Parnalls' involvement with aircraft production can be traced back to the outbreak of World War One when the company came to the notice of the Admiralty as a result of their expertise in wood-working, and in 1915 they awarded Parnalls a number of contracts for the construction of a variety of aircraft types. Consequently, in order to accommodate production a number of premises were rented in Bristol. A factory in Mivart Street, Easton, was used as the aeroplane division's head office and also initially for propeller production, while main assembly was carried in the Coliseum, an old roller-skating rink in Park Row, and experimental work undertaken at Belmont Road, Brislington. In addition, the Quakers Friars site specialised in covering and doping various sub-assemblies.

The completed aircraft were then towed up the road from the Coliseum to the Aircraft Acceptance Park alongside the British & Colonial works at Filton, where they were flown by military test pilots prior to delivery to the RFC and RNAS. Parnalls' production in 1916 was given over exclusively to Short bombers and seaplanes, but for the rest of the war it was the various versions of the Avro '504' trainer, Hamble 'Baby' sea and land planes and Parnell Panther Maritime reconaissance and spotter aircraft that occupied the majority of their time, nearly 860 of these being built before the armistice in 1918.

In 1919, following the cessation of hostilities, Parnalls' existing production contracts were cancelled and the board of W. & T. Avery decided not to continue with aircraft work, but to concentrate their efforts on high-quality shop fitting. George Parnall, the firm's Managing Director, bitterly disagreed and, along with Harold Bolas, resigned and set up in business at the Coliseum Works as George Parnall & Company, an undertaking which was to combine shop fitting with the man-

An aerial view of the Parnall works at Fishponds during the 1950s. Lodge Causeway is in the bottom right hand corner, Parnall Road in the bottom left hand corner.

The Coliseum in Park Row. This building has had an interesting life, being used as not only an aircraft factory by Parnall's but also as a cinema, dance hall, exhibition centre, roller skating rink and a store by Bristol University, before finally being incorporated into a new office development.

ufacture of aircraft. Their first three designs were all naval types, the Parnall 'Puffin' of 1920, the 'Plover' of 1922 and the 'Possom' of 1923, but none of these was awarded production contracts.

During 1923 Parnalls turned their attention to the ultra-light 'Pixie' sports monoplane, but only five of these were built before George Parnall & Company obtained a contract for the refurbishment of 18 de Havilland 'DH 9A' biplanes for the RAF. However, with premises then spread across Bristol and with no airfield of their own, it was

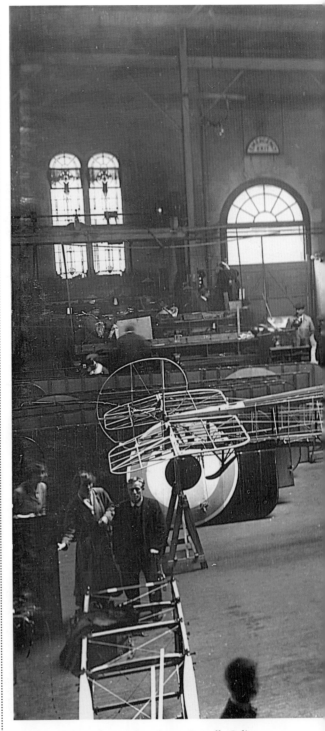

An Avro 504K under construction at Parnalls Coliseum Works in Park Row during World War One.

time for the firm to relocate its aircraft production. This finally took place in 1925 when George Parnall took the opportunity of purchasing the old wartime No.3 (Western) Aircraft Repair Depot at Yate in South Gloucestershire, where the facilities included brick-built engine repair shops,

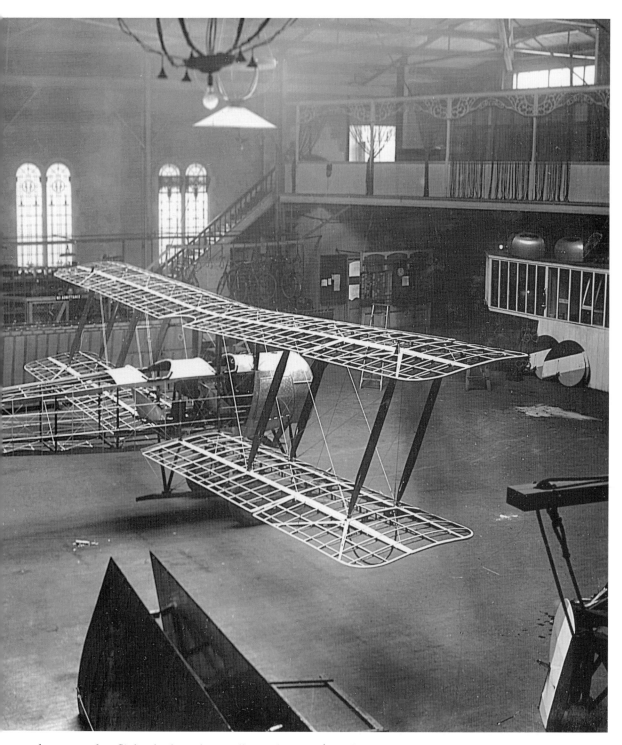

large wooden flight sheds and a small aerodrome. The company then entered the civil light aeroplane market, and after gaining initial experience with the 'Pixie' in 1925 and the 'Imp' in 1927 they exhibited their 'Elf' on Stand 92 at the International Aero Exhibition held at Olympia in 1929.

George Parnall & Company retained its Coliseum Works until 1932 when W & T Avery bought the shop fitting side of the undertaking, which was then transferred to the Fishponds site. In 1935 George Parnall sold his aviation business to Nash & Thompson Ltd of Tolworth in Surrey, a firm that manufactured Frazer-Nash hydraulically-operated aircraft gun turrets, the production of which was subsequently moved to the Yate

Women workers at Parnalls' Coliseum works pose for a photograph in front of Avro 504K wings during World War One.

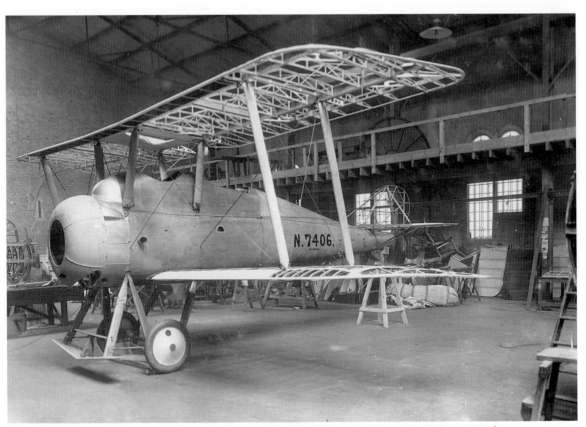

A Parnall Panther maritime reconnaissance and spotter aircraft under construction at the Coliseum Works.

A prototype Parnall Plover fighter outside the Coliseum Works in 1923 at the start of its journey to Filton aerodrome.

site. The company then became Parnall Aircraft Ltd and continued as such until 1945 when, upon being re-titled Parnall (Yate) Ltd., it severed all connections with the aircraft industry. From then on the Yate works concentrated on the production of domestic appliances and by early 2005, after a number of changes of name and ownership, it was being operated by the Indesit Company UK.

The Bristol Aeroplane Company

During World War One many British manufacturers had prospered as a result of the numerous government contracts that had been awarded, but, in order to redress the balance somewhat when war ended, the Treasury introduced what it called Excess Profits Duty. That payment during 1920 forced many fledgling aircraft firms out of business, so in order to keep such duty to a minimum the British & Colonial Aeroplane Company was officially wound up on 9 February 1920 and its fixed assets transferred to the dormant Bristol Aeroplane Company.

The following month the new company took over the development of the Cosmos 'Jupiter' and 'Mercury' engines from the bankrupt Cosmos Engineering Company, and, consequently, Roy Fedden, complete with his designs, 35 staff, and prototype engines, moved from Fishponds to Filton. Here they took up residence in the three hangers built for the wartime Aircraft Acceptance

Park, and in so doing created the West Works, in which was created the nucleus of what was to become the Bristol Aeroplane Company's world famous Aero Engine Division.

For much of the 1920s, apart from the development of a number of prototype machines, practically the only work available for the BAC involved the production and overhaul of small batches of Bristol 'Fighters'. In preparing plans for a peacetime airforce, the Air Ministry began to encourage British manufacturers to begin using all metal construction, and in 1928 this culminated in the Bristol company winning a competition for a day and night fighter.

Known as the Bristol 'Bulldog', this aircraft was in large scale production between 1929 and 1934, during which time nearly 450 of these were built, the vast majority fitted with 'Jupiter' engines. Nevertheless, by 1931 the 'Jupiter' was superseded in production by more advanced 'Mercury' and 'Pegasus' designs, which continued Bristol's tradition of manufacturing some of Britain's finest radial aero engines. Not content with this, Fedden

had also been busy developing sleeve valve engines of a higher potential, and this programme resulted in the appearance of the 'Perseus' in 1932, 'Hercules' in 1935, 'Taurus' in 1936 and 'Centaurus' in 1938.

Although by the end of 1934 the output of engines was higher than ever before, the aircraft works had almost come to a standstill. Nevertheless, this unfortunate situation was not to last long, for in May 1935 the Government at last made the decision to re-equip the RAF with modern equipment and to meet the new challenge, and on 15 June 1935 the Bristol Aeroplane Company Ltd was reorganised as a public limited liability company. Fortunately for the country, Lord Rothermere, proprietor of the 'Daily Mail', had instructed the BAC to build him 'the fastest commercial aeroplane in Europe', and this twin-engined cabin monoplane known as the 'Type 142' had first flown in April 1935.

As it subsequently proved to be some 50mph faster than RAF frontline fighters then in service, his lordship generously presented the aircraft to

Bristol

**sleeve-valve engines
power the majority
of British civil aircraft
in current production**

THE BRISTOL AEROPLANE COMPANY LIMITED · ENGLAND

the nation with the result that the design was adopted by the Air Ministry as the basis for a light-bomber version. Named the 'Blenheim', more than 1,000 had entered service with the RAF before war finally broke out in September 1939. As the Filton works was by this time fully stretched, the production of another Bristol developed aircraft, the 'Bombay' troop carrier, had to be contracted out to Short and Harland Ltd of Belfast.

Very few industries have ever experienced such a terrific boom as that which began for British aircraft manufacturers during the summer of 1935. At that time the BAC had some 4,200 employees, the majority of them working in the engine factory, but within only six months the number stood at 8,233. Likewise, the aircraft works itself, which covered only 13 acres in June 1935, was also greatly extended, and part of this process included the erection on Filton Hill of the separate, single-storey Rodney Works, which was to specialise in cowlings and exhaust systems. In early 1936 the 200,000 square feet East Engine Works was also built on the opposite side of the road to the exist-

An aerial view of the Bristol Aeroplane Company's Filton works as it appeared in 1939.

ing West Works, and shortly after a Shadow Factory for the manufacture of 'Mercury' engines was constructed alongside it at Patchway, this being managed by the company on behalf of the Air Ministry.

All of this of course required a greatly enlarged administration, and April 1936 saw the opening of a new head office block fronting the main Gloucester Road and adjoining the original Filton House. The massive expansion that took place during the second half of the 1930s ensured that at the outbreak of war the BAC complex at Filton covered 2,688,324 square feet on a 732-acre site, making it the largest single aircraft manufacturing unit in the world.

Alongside an improved version of the 'Blenheim', in 1937 the Bristol Aeroplane Company also began manufacturing the 'Beaufort', a general reconnaissance aircraft and torpedo bomber, the first aircraft to standardise sleeve valve engines. The famous cannon-armed, long range, all-weather 'Beaufighter' finally went into production in 1940, by which time, with some 38,000 people on the payroll, the company had overtaken the Imperial Tobacco Company as Bristol's biggest employer. However, from 1943 the number of staff was progressively reduced as workers were redirected to other war priorities such as building tanks, and by the end of the war the Bristol Aeroplane Company was employing just 25,000. The return of peace saw this number fall even further, and by 1950 the company's payroll stood at just 15,000. Although during the period July 1935 until August 1945 the BAC had produced some 12,000 aircraft and over 100,000 engines, half of which had been the ubiquitous 'Hercules', the transition to peace time operations was smoother than back in 1919.

The first project undertaken was the manufacture of a prototype 100-ton, eight-engined airliner with a range of 5,000 miles. However, the first flight of the 'Brabazon' was delayed until 1949, by which time smaller and more economic airliners were operating transatlantic schedules with acceptable regularity. Although this resulted in the cancellation of the project, important les-

Bristol Blenheim Is under construction at the Bristol Aeroplane Company's works at Filton during 1939.

sons learned during its design and manufacture proved invaluable during the development of the smaller 'Britannia' powered by the company's new 'Proteus' turbine engines, a very successful airliner that was produced between 1954 and 1959.

A wartime scene in the canteen at the Bristol Aeroplane Company's Filton Works.

The Bristol Brabazon I under construction in Filton in early 1947.

In the meantime the BAC had also been undertaking the manufacture of another successful aeroplane, the rugged 'Bristol Freighter', a development of the pre-war 'Bombay', and more than 200 of these rolled off the production line at Filton between 1946 and 1958. Other post war projects included setting up a Guided Weapons Department to manufacture the Bristol - Ferranti 'Bloodhound' ground-to-air missile, which entered service in 1957, and the establishment of a Helicopter Department to build Bristol 'Belvedere' and 'Sycamore' helicopters, about 100 of which were made at Filton before such work was transferred to Weston-super-Mare in 1955.

Meanwhile, in 1956 two BAC subsidiary companies were formed, Bristol Aircraft Ltd, which was also responsible for the guided weapons and helicopter divisions, and Bristol Aero-Engines, both of which were wholly owned by the Bristol Aeroplane Company. In the following year the number of employees rose to its post war peak of 28,000, dropping back to 21,000 in 1960, the year in which Bristol Aircraft Ltd was merged with the aerospace interests of Vickers Ltd and the English Electric Company to form the British Aircraft Corporation.

The Filton Division subsequently became responsible for the design and production of the world's first supersonic airliner, 'Concorde', in partnership with the French firm Aerospatiale. A

a sound of victory in the air

Bristol
HERCULES
Engines

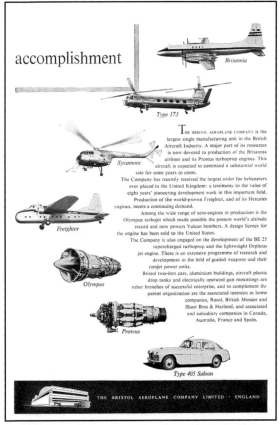

accomplishment

Britannia

Type 173

Sycamore

Freighter

Olympus

Proteus

Type 405 Saloon

THE BRISTOL AEROPLANE COMPANY is the largest single manufacturing unit in the British Aircraft Industry. A major part of its resources is now devoted to production of the Britannia airliner and its Proteus turboprop engines. This aircraft is expected to command a substantial world sale for some years to come.

The Company has recently received the largest order for helicopters ever placed in the United Kingdom: a testimony to the value of eight years' pioneering development work in this important field. Production of the world-proven Freighter, and of its Hercules engines, meets a continuing demand.

Among the wide range of aero-engines in production is the Olympus turbojet which made possible the present world's altitude record and now powers Vulcan bombers. A design licence for the engine has been sold to the United States.

The Company is also engaged on the development of the BE 25 supercharged turboprop and the lightweight Orpheus jet engine. There is an extensive programme of research and development in the field of guided weapons and their ramjet power units.

Bristol two-litre cars, aluminium buildings, aircraft plastic drop tanks and electrically operated gun mountings are other branches of successful enterprise, and to complement the parent organization are the associated interests in home companies, Rotol, British Messier and Short Bros & Harland, and associated and subsidiary companies in Canada, Australia, France and Spain.

THE BRISTOL AEROPLANE COMPANY LIMITED · ENGLAND

The Bristol Aeroplane Company
Limited points with pride to a
forty-year record of steady progress
achieved largely by the encouragement of individual thought and
enterprise among its workers.

THE *Bristol* AEROPLANE CO. LTD · ENGLAND

903

A WORLD FORCE IN AVIATION

BRITISH AIRCRAFT CORPORATION is one of the industry's most powerful organisations. It has research, design, development and production teams which have made the Corporation world leaders in civil and military aircraft and in guided missiles. Behind the Corporation stand the great parent industrial groups of Vickers, English Electric and Bristol Aeroplane Company. In skills and ability, in equipment and achievement, British Aircraft Corporation has a high reputation—with a big job to do now and in the years that lie ahead.

BRITISH AIRCRAFT CORPORATION
FILTON BRISTOL

With the Concorde supersonic airliner, Britain and France lead the world.

Leading the British programme on Concorde—designed, developed and manufactured in collaboration with Sud-Aviation—is the Filton Division of

BRITISH AIRCRAFT CORPORATION

AC 94   ONE HUNDRED PALL MALL LONDON SW1

ture of aero engines. Further winds of change blew through Filton on 1 January 1978 when British Aerospace, a nationalised corporation, was created by the amalgamation of the British Aircraft Corporation, Hawker-Siddeley Aircraft, Hawker-Siddeley Dynamics and Scottish Aviation. However, public ownership was only a temporary measure, for at the beginning of 1981 it became British Aerospace plc, a public limited company. Sadly, this actually marked the end of the Bristol works as a builder of complete aircraft, the last 'Concorde' having been delivered in June 1980.

The break-up of the old Bristol Aeroplane company saw the disappearance of the famous Bristol name, and since the early 1980s the Filton complex has been given over to construction of sub-assemblies to be used by other manufacturers, or for conversion and refurbishment work. Nevertheless, by adapting the pattern of work to the ever changing market place this has ensured that, unlike a number of Bristol's other historic concerns, British Aerospace and Rolls-Royce are continuing a tradition for quality and excellence that has epitomised Bristol-designed and manufactured products over a period of many centuries.

similar fate also befell Bristol Aero-Engines Ltd, which in 1959 had merged with Armstrong-Siddeley Engines to form Bristol-Siddeley Engines Ltd, a company which lasted only until 1966 when it was finally acquired by Rolls-Royce to become their Bristol Engine Division. Although they subsequently closed the Rodney Works at Filton, Rolls-Royce plc continued production at Patchway, where today they still employ a substantial number of local people in the manufac-

The Bristol Aeroplane Company's old Art Deco headquarters building, photographed empty and awaiting an uncertain future in 2001.

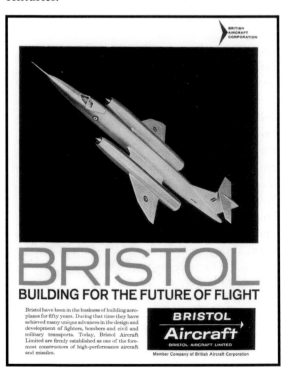

BRISTOL
BUILDING FOR THE FUTURE OF FLIGHT

Bristol have been in the business of building aeroplanes for fifty years. During that time they have achieved many unique advances in the design and development of fighters, bombers and civil and military transports. Today, Bristol Aircraft Limited are firmly established as one of the foremost constructors of high-performance aircraft and missiles.

BRISTOL
Aircraft
BRISTOL AIRCRAFT LIMITED

Member Company of British Aircraft Corporation

Company Index